Contents

Editorial

Maree Keating

As consumers and workers we are all intimately familiar with the everyday notions of trade that govern our lives. And yet, the rules and agreements that comprise the global 'free trade' system seem remote to most of us. It is not just liberal economists who find it difficult to use a gendered analysis of trade. The issues and the debates are complex and take time to consider. Yet the 'free trade' system is a gender-related issue for at least two immediately obvious reasons. First, it relies on gender inequalities in order to fuel the engines of production with a supply of cheap, exploitable labour. Second, trade rules and agreements affect the way in which national priorities are set, and they have an impact on gender equality.

In meeting the diverse demands of populations, governments, and companies everywhere for manufactured goods, agricultural produce, raw materials, technology, services, knowledge, and medicines, the current trade system divides the world into global consumers and global suppliers of common goods and services. Individual nations are compelled to adopt a 'liberal' economic model in order to be part of the trading regime. This model requires countries to prioritise the development of export products which can compete globally, rather than focus on local self-sufficiency measures which promote maximum employment, or human-development opportunities for the population.

Over the past two decades, international finance institutions (IFIs) have encouraged developing countries to accept economic measures such as structural adjustment policies (SAPs), to assist them to become part of the global economy. These measures require them, among other things, to pare down domestic expenditure on social welfare, publicly funded health and education services, water and fuel, and focus on increasing national income through export production, fee collection for service provision, or privatisation.

The global trading system assumes the possibility of a level playing field. It relies on the notion of a common global economy, from which all can equally benefit by following the same rules. Increasingly since the 1980s, the rules of trade have promoted the easy or 'free' movement of goods and services across national borders, to facilitate global supply. At the present time, the growth of this free movement, the central concept of trade liberalisation, is a process reliant on, and reinforcing of, unequal gender roles. It is a process capable of having gendered impacts on human and social development. The editors of *Gender and Development* Volume 11 No. 1 (2003: 5), on the theme of 'Women Reinventing Globalisation', noted that, while 'the WTO is supposed to create equal opportunities for all economies in the global market place, in fact "free trade" is a misnomer'. The global trade system incurs costs. The

Gender, Development, and Trade

The books in Oxfam's *Focus on Gender* series were originally published as single issues of the journal *Gender and Development*, which is published by Routledge Publishing, an imprint of Taylor and Francis, on behalf of Oxfam three times a year. It is the only European journal to focus specifically on gender and development issues internationally, to explore the links between gender and development initiatives, and to make the links between theoretical and practical work in this field. For information about journal subscription rates, please apply to Routledge Publishing, T & F Customer Services, T & F Informa UK Ltd., Sheepen Place, Colchester, Essex, OC3 3LP, UK. Tel: +44 (0) 207 017 5544; Fax: +44 (0) 207 017 5198.

Gender and Development is also published on-line. For further details, visit the Taylor and Francis website at www.tandf.co.uk/journals, or the Oxfam website at www.oxfam.org.uk/go/gad

The views expressed in this book are those of the individual contributors, and not necessarily those of the Editor or publisher.

Front cover: *Nioka Abbott, a banana farmer and Chair of the Langley Park Fair Trade Group, Windward Islands. Changes in supermarket policies threaten their livelihoods.*
Photo: Abigail Hadeed/Oxfam

authors in this current collection help us to identify who carries those costs, and how.

How the WTO works

The World Trade Organisation was established, with around 150 member states, in 1995, as a result of the Uruguay round of trade negotiations, held under the General Agreement on Tariffs and Trade (GATT). The purpose of the WTO is to regulate, administer, and arbitrate on the rules of international trade. Member states agree unanimously to most decisions, legislating them afterwards in their parliaments. Trade decisions are made in a number of forums, but mainly in the Ministerial meetings, held every two years. Few women attend these forums, or have a role in the decision-making processes. The rules of the WTO work in the interests of a global trade community, although at the Doha Ministerial meeting in 2001 recognition of the needs and priorities of developing countries were set out in a range of issues relating to special and differential treatment. The failure of Northern countries, however, to respect the interests of the South by agreeing to special and differential treatment was precisely the cause of the breakdown of the negotiations in the Cancun Ministerial meeting in 2003. Mariama Williams explains what happened in her contribution to this collection.

WTO rules are enshrined in trade agreements between nations or blocks of nations, and breaches are dealt with by WTO panels. This makes the WTO a potent global instrument, with more power to enforce global standards than, say, the United Nations. The lack of women representatives at every level of decision making within the WTO is a critical issue, given the stated aim in US and EU trade policy to 'mainstream' gender throughout trade agreements. If it is not possible to address women's interests at the highest levels of trade negotiations, it is hard to see how they can be addressed at more pressurised levels, involving resource-poor countries, further down the chain.

Current negotiations in North–South trade agreements put pressure on developing countries to surrender to the interests of the North, in ways detrimental to the most vulnerable populations. Women, routinely at the bottom of the social and economic chain, are the most vulnerable to these shifts in policy and practice, as Marceline White and others explain here. Trade partners are increasingly obliged to develop export specialities which meet consumer demand at the cheapest price, and in the fastest time. They are also increasingly expected to allow the import of foreign goods and services, which can be more efficiently provided by more powerful trade partners. In order to 'free' the wholesale movement of goods and services, trade 'liberalisation' measures can be imposed on the weaker parties. In effect this means that national policies, tariffs, or protections that are perceived to inhibit the free flow of trade into or out of a country can be overruled.

In effect, there are many ways in which WTO rules protect Northern markets and jobs, while making it impossible for Southern markets to protect theirs. Williams describes how 'competition policy', currently under discussion, could force poor nations to surrender local contracts to foreign companies, to the detriment of local businesses, many of which are owned by women. Flynn and Kofman describe how WTO rules favour the North in the regulation of movement of persons across borders for the purpose of work, to the detriment of women workers in the South.

The range of goods and services covered by WTO trade rules has, over the past few years, expanded from agricultural and manufactured goods to include patents on intellectual property, such as new plant breeds, medicinal combinations, or traditional designs, as well as the movement of workers across borders, and basic service provision including water, health, and education services. This expansion of terms introduces new, gendered consequences for the South. Suman Sahai illustrates these consequences by describing the impact of rules on the patenting of plant breeds and medicinal knowledge in Asia.

The rules of trade are not neutral

Every two years, the trade ministers from WTO member states meet to discuss and agree on rules of trade at the Ministerial meetings. The terms of trade are currently weighted in favour of the developed countries, which are seeking ever greater access to Southern markets for their subsidised goods and value-added services.

Over the past decade, a rapid growth in world trade has been made possible through changes in technology, transportation, tele-communications, and the transfer of goods. The success of individuals, companies, and nations during the course of these changes has relied on their capacity to predict consumer demand, relocate, and diversify or change products at short notice.

Workforce 'flexibility' has become the foundation for success in meeting these demands. To stay competitive, companies need to be able to increase or reduce the size of their workforces and the rates of pay, depending on constantly changing profit margins and pressure from buyers further up the chain. If they cannot succeed in this, they run the risk of losing their global niche. Women are the main recruits to new forms of casual work in the manufacturing industry worldwide, and Annie Delaney, Thalia Kidder, and Kate Raworth describe the negative impact of flexibility requirements on them.

Changes in the way in which trade agreements are fixed have affected every aspect of national development, including the positions of women and men in relation to it. Governments have a vested interest in helping their companies stay competitive. Legislation and policies which interfere with free trade and flexible work arrangements are modified, often amounting to the weakening of protections for local populations, and particularly against the interests of women workers.

Trade and gender equality

There is a 'chorus of critique' (Van Staveren, 2002) from NGOs, academics, and govern-ments concerning the pace of economic globalisation and its impacts on human rights, labour standards, biodiversity, environment, and gender equality. Inequal-ities between nation states and the WTO, between buyers and suppliers in trade agreements, and between men and women in the workplace have been key deter-minants of the beneficiaries of the current trade regime. There has been, as contributor Mariama Williams notes, a two-way connection between gender and trade liberalisation. Trade liberalisation can increase or decrease gender inequality, and gender inequality can determine the success or failure of the trade-liberalisation project.

Liberalisation policies have had negative impacts on poor people all over the world, and women have carried the greatest burden of these impacts. This, in turn, can add to gender discrimination and inequality. In many countries, the cost of living has increased and social spending has decreased, resulting in more unpaid work for women in the provision of family health care, education, water collection, and transport of household goods. Access to basic services has declined, as have nutritional standards, with particularly negative impacts on women and girls.

Instead of benefiting from trade liberalisation, rural women have often lacked the resources necessary to adjust to changes in export production and have thus lost livelihoods. Their opportunities to diversify into occupations or markets requiring land, mobility, or resources are often severely limited, due to the social restrictions and the discrimination that women face in society. Urban women, on the other hand, have in many cases gained precarious, poorly paid jobs in factories, with conditions which compromise the care that they can give themselves and their families. This incurs a range of social costs, which girls and women often have to pay.

WTO Ministerial meetings have become forums at which civil society organisations and governments of developing nations alike insist that these impacts be taken into consideration. In preparation for these and other trade-negotiation forums, gender and trade advocates are undertaking a re-examination of the impacts of trade, through the use of gender-differentiated research indicators and tools.

The evidence suggests that any economic benefits of liberalisation measures to poor countries so far have heavily relied on preferential treatment by Northern partners. This has taken the form of special arrangements, where export goods from poor countries have had access to markets in Northern countries, without Southern countries having to return trade privileges. As discussed by Karin Ulmer, economic partnership agreements, currently under re-negotiation between the EU and Africa, propose the introduction of reciprocal trade rights, which will allow the free flow of subsidised EU agricultural products into Africa. This brings with it a high risk of overwhelming local suppliers and producers, and destroying local livelihoods in vulnerable sectors, where women predominate.

The Multifibre Agreement between the USA and several textile-producing countries in Asia provides an example of the importance of 'special treatment'. This agreement has provided a set annual quota for textiles entering the USA from Asia, thus providing Southern countries with a regular, guaranteed market for their goods and corresponding employment for thousands of women. With this agreement now ending, and with China taking over much of the global production in textiles, the economic situation for poor women, who have been dependent on the new manufacturing boom,

will worsen in many countries unless some quotas with the USA are maintained.

Articles in this collection

The articles collected here deal with two overarching concerns. First, in what ways do gender and other social inequalities work together to support and facilitate the unsustainable 'race to the bottom' which now characterises the global supply system? And second, is it possible for a global trading system to work as part of an international regime of rules and standards that could reduce poverty and simultaneously increase equality and opportunities for women? In addressing these and other related questions, the contributors have pointed us towards research and action which is being taken by unions, governments, trade negotiators, corporations, academics, and NGOs. If trade agreements are to be compatible with broader social and gender equity goals in the pursuit of sustainable national development, Marzia Fontana (Fontana, Joekes, Masika, 1998: 27) reminds us that 'the challenge is… to identify and promote the conditions and patterns of trade most beneficial to women and likely to extend their gains into the longer term'.

This collection includes contributions from academics, policy advisers, and trade-union campaigners, who discuss how current trends in international trade regimes affect the security, status, income, and self-esteem of women. Whether in cross-border migration-for-work schemes in The Philippines, rural communities of tribal India, clothing factories in China, home work in Australia, food processing in Mozambique, or cut flower and maize sectors in Zimbabwe, women and their labour are intrinsic to the scaling up of global trade.

Our writers discuss the application of new evidence, tools, and strategies in organising workers, lobbying companies, and influencing governments and trade decision makers to consider gendered impacts of trade. We read about successful union campaigns, emerging corporate models based on long-term development partnerships, and successful lobbying of the US government following the application of gender-sensitive trade-impact assessments. Contributors tell us that we can quantify the hidden costs of global supply chains to women workers, and use research into the gendered impact of trade agreements to exert a positive influence on policy in the North.

At the national level we learn how women entrepreneurs are surviving the competition in Botswana, and how the precarious labour regime under which women work in Shenzhen, China, is facilitated by the global 'race to the bottom', as well as other local factors. And at the global level we read about directions for further research in relation to the 2005 WTO Ministerial meeting, and the gender-related dimensions of controversial regulations due for discussion at that forum.

Women workers fuel growth in global trade and carry the cost

Economic research can tell us seemingly contradictory things about the relationship between gender inequality and economic development, depending on the indicators used. Seguino, in her cross-country research, reveals that in countries experiencing industrial growth, the higher the difference between men and women's wages, the higher the Gross Domestic Product. She concludes that gender inequality can be construed as good for economic growth, because of the low level of women's wages (Van Stevern, 2002). But economic growth, defined within short-term financial parameters, goes against the desirable social outcomes in national development planning, which in turn affects overall affluence. Other research shows, for instance, that where gender inequality in education and health

care leads to lower life expectancy, overall GDP is ultimately reduced.

Due to their primary role as care-givers, women often seek flexible economic pursuits, such as small trade or casual work. Peggy Ntseane's account of life for small businesswomen demonstrates that, while small business is a niche which attracts a huge number of poor Botswana women, survival is made difficult for business-women by gender discrimination, and very few of those who set up a business ever succeed in expanding it. In addition, gender roles bind women to particular ways of working with each other for survival. In a traditional society such as Botswana, with strong gender-role segregation, maintenance of family, social, and business networks is an important ingredient of women's survival in business. While a strategy of collaboration ensures that extended families profit from women's business involvement, this same strategy often militates against competitive business outcomes for women. Ntseane's article raises questions about the appropriateness of trade competitiveness as a strategy which can benefit poor women in small and medium-sized enterprises.

Increasingly casualised work conditions, where companies offer no contracts, set hours, overtime payments, or other conditions, have gone hand in hand with the 'feminisation' of manufacturing industries. Several contributors point out the growing convergence of women's social and economic vulnerability and industry's needs for flexible workers in the new global trade chains. Worldwide, women pre-dominate in the expanding areas of home work and informalised factory work because they are often bound by their domestic obligations to take work that is offered close to home. Others, who can escape domestic responsibilities, work as semi-skilled and unskilled migrant labourers, fulfilling the need for domestic labour in the affluent North, or working in special economic zones to produce goods for export. Poor women work in some of the world's most precarious migrant jobs, often temporarily fuelling the 'engine for economic growth' back home by providing a cheap and flexible labour force elsewhere, and ensuring that money remitted home is spent wisely, on health care and education for their families.

Research outlined in this issue shows how gender biases in workplaces still characterise women as more 'suited to' unskilled work. Nazneen Kanji's article points out that in cashew-nut processing factories in Mozambique, women work longer hours and earn less than men, as men predominate in the higher-paid areas of work. Even in companies experimenting with providing better conditions and work practices, conventional assumptions about women's capacities exclude them from better-paid work as well as representation higher up the chain. Due to the combination of gender discrimination and their domestic responsibilities, women are often forced to accept the most insecure jobs, in workplaces offering little or no bargaining space and bad conditions. Annie Delaney describes the global trend for women to fill the ranks of the growing informalised labour force as home workers, fruit pickers, construction workers, call-centre workers, street vendors, and casual factory workers. She describes how the invisibility and lack of legal and union protection for home workers makes them particularly vulnerable to unethical corporate practices. The ease with which workers can be recruited and fired, she says, is a vital element of companies' ability to maintain global competitiveness, concluding that 'The redefinition of a worker's relationship to the factory is a critical component to attracting and maintaining foreign customers.'

Delaney agrees with Kidder and Raworth that one way of developing better corporate practice is for unions and government to work together in setting and enforcing basic standards for workers. In working towards a greater acceptance of the Homeworker Code, which sets minimum standards for home workers, unions in various countries, including Australia, are working with both government and corporate parties to induce companies to meet decent standards for home workers.

Kidder and Raworth argue in their article that the hidden costs that women incur in these new, casualised jobs far outweigh the benefits gained. They explain how the weakening of government labour legislation and enforcement, combined with increasing demands from buyers and correlated corporate practices, and gender discrimination in the broader society, work together to create an exploitative and precarious working life for women in the global trade chain. They go further, to suggest the ways in which society carries the costs, while companies benefit from exploitative work practices. Their article illustrates the ways in which we can actually count long-term costs to society in terms of lower health standards and fragmented social networks, unpaid work in the home, gender inequality, and overall economic insecurity. They present a matrix which, they claim, can ultimately be used in 'estimating the future public health costs of failing to enforce laws on health and safety at work today, or by estimating the government revenue forgone – and the health or education it could have paid for – by providing tax holidays to foreign investors today'.

Pun Ngai describes the multiple trends that have created a system of precarious and unprotected work for Chinese women. China's membership of the WTO has implications for workers, buyers, and sellers worldwide, because of its size and its capacity to produce a huge volume of the cheap manufactured goods required by the world's markets. It is easy to concentrate on the impact of China on the trade system, rather than the other way around.

Pun Ngai's piece takes us into the Shenzhen special economic zone, where a three-tiered set of practices creates a new, precarious employment system for Chinese women. On the one level there are the practices of international buyers, which provide incentives to increase production and profit margins but do not seriously apply codes to worker conditions in supplier companies. Second, national and provincial Chinese laws do not provide the most basic citizenship rights for non-resident rural migrant workers in transnational companies. Chinese subcontractors benefit from these legally approved conditions and provide exploitative conditions for workers, relying on informal worker networks to take up the recruitment, discipline, and training of workers. Workers without citizenship rights in the city, and who are dependent on informal family networks to survive, are not in a position to organise or challenge the *status quo*. Finally, underpinning the whole system is the ready supply of willing female workers. Changing gender relations in rural China provide an exploitable, young female workforce, whose members are eager to earn money and increase their bargaining power in the years of 'freedom' before marriage.

WTO and gender equality

The Convention on the Elimination of All Forms of Discrimination Against Women (CEDAW), the International Labour Organisation, the Convention on Biological Diversity, as well as other well-supported international instruments, set out rules on how governments must protect vulnerable people and environments. While they are not enforceable in the way that trade agreements are, they can help to apply pressure on signatories to respect basic standards.

Marceline White reminds us in her article that 'As the purview of trade agreements has expanded, so too, have the concerns of civil society organisations. Trade agreements now affect areas that once seemed far removed, such as environmental protection, labour rights and working conditions, sustainable development, and gender equality'. While gender-differentiated dimensions of economic development are still not addressed

in trade discussions, environmental and labour standards as well as human rights and gender equality are increasingly situated within the ambit of global trade negotiations. Global trade rules and agreements which directly or indirectly require trade partners to contravene socially conscious national legislation or policy, and international conventions, can erode women's rights.

In the analysis presented by Suman Sahai, for example, current trade agreements on plant varieties and biological materials run the risk of contravening international conventions and treaties which acknowledge the central role of women in preserving plant diversity, as well as threatening national policies protecting natural resources, the environment, and indigenous people's rights. Where plant breeders are granted individual rights to patent and own plant varieties, this contravenes global agreements which acknowledge community ownership of biological material and collective benefit-sharing from biodiversity. In many agreements, plant breeding must fit in with WTO criteria, set out in trade agreements, which Southern farmers can rarely meet. As women in Asia are primarily responsible for selection and breeding of plant stock, their roles and livelihoods are directly affected by such trade agreements.

White takes up similar points in her discussion of the impact of free trade agreements between the USA and Mexico. She explains that, despite strong national regulations in Mexico, the constitutional rights of indigenous peoples in Mexico are not recognised under the North American Free Trade Agreement (NAFTA). This threatens indigenous women's rights over intellectual property, such as potentially lucrative traditional designs. And, despite strong national labour laws, trade sanctions cannot be used by Mexico in response to exploitation or sexual harassment of women workers employed by foreign companies. Even though the law protects Mexican women workers from exploitative treatment, they do not have recourse to this law when working for transnational companies in Mexico's Export Processing Zones.

Should WTO have the power?

Several of the authors question whether the WTO should be able to determine rules governing such a wide range of issues. One of the crucial questions arising from this discussion is whether it is desirable for the WTO to have the power to enforce global standards on all social, labour, and environmental issues, as they intersect with the transfer of goods and services worldwide. While some argue that this would give too much power to the WTO, which should deal solely with trade matters, others see it as a useful strategy for enforcing standards, including those on gender discrimination and labour conditions, through binding agreements. This will be a key issue for campaigners over the next few years, and particularly in the lead-up to the next Ministerial meeting in 2005.

The controversial trade rules under negotiation in the current WTO talks have implications for gender equality. For example, discussions covering cross-border move - ment of persons for work focus mainly on professionals, most likely to be moving from a developed to a developing country for purposes of highly paid technical work. Developed countries do not acknowledge the high demand in the North for semi-skilled female domestic workers from the South, or the importance of these remittances to Southern economies. As noted by Flynn and Kofman, the ensuing lack of formal travel and employment agreements for semi-skilled and unskilled workers increases the vulnerability of women migrants to trafficking networks and exploitation.

Mariama Williams provides a summary of the key issues for discussion in the WTO since 2001, and conveys the gender implications of what can appear to be gender-neutral trade issues. One example is the issue of procurement. Currently under debate in the WTO is regulation of the documentation and other standards that companies use in the procurement of equipment. Improvements in procurement systems are costly, and if companies in developing countries were unable to meet these standards, governments would not be permitted to do business with them. This would have a devastating impact on local businesses in developing countries and open up the developing world to companies from wealthier countries. WTO regulations that enforce high procurement standards on local companies would automatically exclude small to medium-sized enterprise (SME) operators in many developing countries, previously receiving preferential treatment on government purchases. This would have a direct impact on women, who predominate in small to medium-sized enterprises. Williams explains how the national expense associated with implementing procurement policies can also force poor nations to shave further costs from their domestic budgets, resulting in a reduced overall basic services expenditure, and ultimately leading to heavier burdens for women in the unpaid areas of domestic care.

It is not just rules determined at the WTO which can influence gender equality, but also clauses within cross-regional trade agreements. Ulmer argues that, if the economic partnership agreements between EU and the African, Caribbean, and Pacific states are renegotiated to allow subsidised goods from the EU to flood local markets, it is very likely that local producers will be unable to compete, and that women in a range of sectors will be hit particularly hard by the drop in employment and income. Research from Zimbabwe already shows the heavy negative impact of such agreements on women working in the cut flower, sugar, beef, and cereal sectors. Zimbabwean women who currently enjoy employment through lively trade with other African countries will lose these markets to the EU, unless regional countries continue to give preferential treatment to each other through regional alliances.

Future directions on gender and trade

All of the authors show how research and action can be used to encourage a re-thinking of trade practices that are damaging to women. Gender-sensitive research parameters, as well as tools for determining overall gains and losses for women and men, are now available to trade decision makers. Perhaps the two most interesting tools under discussion in this issue are the matrix for counting the cost of precarious work, described by Kidder and Raworth, and the Trade Impact Review (TIR) framework described by White. While the matrix of hidden costs has many potential applications in campaigns aimed at companies and workers, the TIR has already been applied in the Mexican context, and the results successfully used by the Women's Edge Coalition to influence US trade policy.

The 'mapping project' described in Delaney's article demonstrates the value of developing global alliances between factory workers and home workers in the same supply chain, and she also demonstrates how global campaigns can make potent use of existing labour codes to pressure governments and companies to observe minimum standards.

Research done by organisations such as APRODEV on trade-agreement impacts in Zimbabwe and by IIED on the impacts of trade liberalisation in Mozambique are shown to be of use in regional trade forums to assist governments and civil society to develop arguments for gender-aware trade agreements. Many governments have already developed their own alternatives to the limited options available on biological patenting, and other issues, in response to the Northern bias in trade discussions.

Ulmer's proposition is that regional alliances between Southern states offer a crucial opportunity to developing countries to stand their ground in trade bargaining. It is in the interests of women in the South that their livelihoods, operating at the levels of local and cross-border trade, are protected. Regional agreements between Southern states could provide this protection, and add a regional voice to the negotiating table, which is currently dominated by the interests of developed countries.

Advocates of gender equality in trade are preparing inputs to the 2005 WTO Ministerial in Hong Kong, and are developing policy positions on rules and agreements governing issues such as the position of women migrant workers and intellectual property rights, as well as agricultural agreements and other issues as they affect women, women's rights, and gender relations.

The contributors to this volume inform us of strategies that are capable of challenging the notion that 'free' trade is fair and gender-neutral. Alliances are being built between unions and women working as casual labourers, home workers, and factory workers in global chains. Consumer demands for non-exploitative practices are influencing corporate standards in the North. Governments are responding to lobbying on codes of conduct and trade-impact assessments. And models of better practice in business are demonstrating that fair and equitable corporate practice can work for business and workers alike.

However, more work needs to be done on trade agreements to ensure that they benefit women and men equally. The authors remind us that it is important to exert leverage at all the points in the global chain, so that profits are not being made by brand-name companies at the expense of women workers. Further research is needed in many areas, including the gender-related effects in the most vulnerable sectors of international trade. Further research could examine the correlation between aspects of trade policy and positive changes in the bases for women's disadvantage, or gender inequities in the divisions of labour. Using this research, the EU and the USA may be in a better position to put their gender-mainstreaming policies into practice in trade agreements.

At the level of the WTO, where trade rules are determined, the question remains: where does a trade rule start and stop, and where does it interconnect with rules governing human rights? For, if rules made in the WTO can and do have negative impacts on gender equality, it is incumbent upon trade-policy decision makers to find ways to fully address these potential impacts at every point of trade negotiations.

References

Fontana M., S. Joekes, and R. Masika (1998) 'Global Trade Expansion and Liberalisation: Gender Issues and Impacts', BRIDGE, University of Sussex, Institute of Development Studies.

van Staveren, I. (2002) 'Towards Monitoring Mutual Trade – Gender Links', The Hague: Institute of Social Studies.

'Good jobs' and hidden costs:
women workers documenting the price of precarious employment

Thalia Kidder and Kate Raworth[1]

This article describes the precarious terms and conditions of employment experienced by millions of women working in global supply chains in the food and garment industries, and describes the main forces leading to that precariousness. It then presents a typology of costs and determinants of precarious employment, in the form of a matrix, which serves as an analytical framework for documenting the hidden costs borne by women workers. Thirdly, the article presents some of the approaches used by Oxfam International and partner organisations to make calculations of those costs, including the challenges encountered. Lastly, the article suggests several ways in which the matrix could be used and some ideas for further research.

It has been frequently claimed that women workers are among the winners of globalisation. *'In praise of cheap labour: bad jobs at bad wages are better than no jobs at all'* wrote the economist Paul Krugman, in response to critiques of employment terms and conditions in garment factories around the world (Krugman 1997, 1). Employed at the end of chains that supply fresh produce and garments to major retailers, many are earning cash incomes for the first time and often earning more than they would in alternative employment opportunities.

But there are often hidden costs for women who are employed in these labour-intensive trading sectors, because they are employed in precarious ways. Many are repeatedly hired on short-term contracts, paid by piece rate, lack social security or employment benefits, face long and erratic hours, and are at risk of sudden job loss. Poor management or gender relations have typically been blamed for precarious conditions; however, two other significant factors are shaping employment conditions:

the sourcing and purchasing practices of retailers who demand low-cost, fast, and flexible production in their supply chains, and government policies and practices aiming to make the labour force more 'flexible' to meet these retailers' needs.

As part of an ongoing international campaign to 'Make Trade Fair', Oxfam International undertook research with partner organisations in 12 countries as a basis for campaigning for the rights of workers employed in global fresh-produce and garment supply chains. More than 1,300 workers – mostly women – were interviewed, as well as around 130 farm and factory managers, 50 supply-chain agents, 50 NGO and government officials, and 17 retail company representatives.

The aim was to produce evidence of the costs borne by workers as a result of retailers' sourcing and purchasing practices, and governments' labour policies and practices. In particular, we aimed to show the costs not only of poor working conditions but of insecure terms of employment which are shaped by the above factors. The motivation to make these costs explicit was threefold:

1 To reveal how workers are bearing the costs of being employed in supply chains which demand greater speed and flexibility, and how government policies weaken, or fail to enforce, national labour laws. Women workers effectively provide a subsidy to production under this business model, and pay the price of government trade strategies that rely on precarious jobs.

2 To provide policy makers with a fuller account of the monetary and non-monetary costs incurred by workers as a result of flexible labour-market policies and practices – in the same way that feminist economics has made calculations of the value of unpaid work, and environmental economics has estimated the costs of environmental degradation.

3 To provide women workers' organisations with an approach for systematically identifying these costs, so that they can propose ways of removing or reducing them, and hold decision-makers accountable.[2]

Precarious employment in global supply chains

In both rich and poor countries, women are the ones who cut, sew, and pack clothing, pick and pack fruit, prune and cut flowers. Women constitute 65 per cent of the factory workforce in the Honduran garment industry, 85 per cent in Bangladesh, and 90 per cent in Cambodia. In the cut flower industry, women hold 65 per cent of the jobs in Colombia and 87 per cent in Zimbabwe. In the fruit industry, women constitute 69 per cent of temporary and seasonal workers in South Africa, and 52 per cent in Chile, while women hold only 26 per cent and 5 per cent of the long-term jobs in these countries, respectively. Ninety per cent of home-based workers in the UK

are women (Dolan and Sorby 2003; Oxfam International 2004).

Women's over-representation in labour-intensive industries, and in the more precarious jobs within them, can be attributed to several factors. First, some factory and farm managers adhere to gender-stereotyped ideas that women employees are more dextrous for this 'hand work', more 'flexible' about performing endless repetitive and unskilled tasks, or more 'docile' and therefore less likely to make demands.

Second, more women than men may apply for precarious jobs: women's family responsibilities may leave them unable to turn down daily or temporary jobs, while men may travel in search of better opportunities. Likewise, seasonal or home work may produce fewer conflicts with women's family duties.

Third, the myth persists that women's jobs provide 'extra' income, perpetuating the rationale that it is less important for them to have a stable job, employment benefits, training opportunities, or promotion. In fact, our research affirmed that benefits such as paid leave time, health and maternity coverage, and regular hours are highly valued by women workers because it is precisely those benefits that enable them to balance their paid work with the responsibilities imposed upon them by gender roles for unpaid caring work in the home.

Lastly, women are over-represented in these jobs because there are few better alternatives available to them. '*May God bless the flowers, because they provide us with work,*' say the women in Colombia's flower greenhouses (Oxfam International 2004, 16). Burdened by school costs and medical expenses, women in poor families increasingly depend on earning cash incomes. Many hope to escape rural poverty, declining agricultural incomes, or subordinated family roles, migrating across provinces and countries to do so. And the crisis of HIV and

AIDS makes some families all the more dependent on those who can work, increasing the need for their caring work too.

For many individual women, their jobs on farms and in factories have facilitated personal empowerment, and in some cases economic independence or greater equality in the household. But though these jobs are valued, they too frequently result in precarious terms of employment. Our research found workers' experiences of insecurity, excessive stress, and subordination particularly widespread among the women workers, the vast majority of whom are also the primary caregivers in the family.

Insecurity is a critical issue: women hired repeatedly on short-term contracts provide their employers with the expertise of permanent workers, while systematically being denied access to the benefits of long-term employees. Erratic and excessive overtime forces women to rearrange childcare at short notice, often while being underpaid for these hours. Excessive stress is endemic, and short-term gains turn into long-term losses for workers who get burned out, often ending up with short working lives. Women are typically subordinated through segregation into the low-paid, low-skill jobs, sexual harassment, or intimidation for involvement in union organising.

These factors interact with and exacerbate one another. Workers on insecure contracts have weaker bargaining positions in the workplace, are less able to demand their rights, and are more exposed to excessive production pressures, intimidation, and harassment.

Forces shaping precarious employment

What are the causes of these precarious terms and conditions of employment? Commonly cited and significant causes include gender stereotypes and poor farm and factory management. Yet two other forces play an increasingly influential role:

the purchasing practices of retailers, and governments' labour policies. Food and clothing retailers source their products through extensive global supply chains, with a very strong negotiating position over their suppliers. This enables them to dictate terms and conditions of supply and to create the low-cost, flexible supply chain that they seek. Farm and factory managers interviewed in our research confirmed the increasing pressure from retailers in demanding faster production at shorter notice, more flexibility in order size and spacing, higher quality standards, and tighter specification of the inputs to be used – all at stagnant or falling prices. In the Sri Lankan garment industry, for example, production times have typically fallen from 90 to 45 days over the last three years, while prices to some suppliers have fallen 35 per cent in 18 months (Oxfam International 2004).

Employers in turn pass these pressures on to their workers (Figure 1). Demands for faster delivery – enforced through fines for missing deadlines – turn into excessive overtime for workers, who are forced to stay until the order is completed. 'We have a very young workforce of women,' explained one garment factory manager in Morocco. 'At times the women have to stay up working all night, and they understand perfectly the need for that flexibility' (Oxfam International 2004, 53). Likewise, falling prices are passed on to workers in the form of high production targets and low piece-rate pay; erratic and short-notice orders result in short-term hiring for workers. In effect, the flexibility gained by retailers at the top of the chain results in precarious employment for the women at the bottom of it.

Government policies and practices are too often geared to accommodating, rather than preventing, these excessive supply-chain pressures. Many governments routinely fail to implement existing labour laws, either constrained by a lack of resources or desirous of creating more flexible labour

Figure 1: Supply-chain pressures create precarious employment

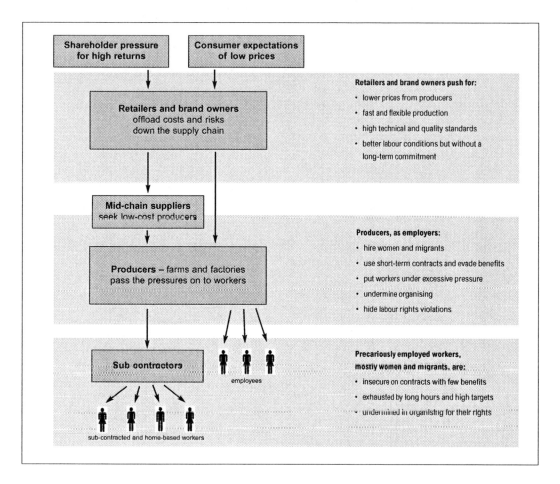

practices without changing the law. One labour inspector in Bangalore's garment factories told researchers, 'We have received instructions from above to be lenient in these inspections, as these factories are contributing to the economic growth of the state' (Oxfam International 2004, 63). The failure to protect trade union rights, and sometimes their active sabotage, is particularly damaging, since it undermines workers' ability to defend their rights themselves.

Some governments weaken national labour laws to make the labour market more 'flexible' through easier hiring and firing, extended limits on overtime, and increasing the use of temporary contracts. This trend is

effectively converting once-illegal excesses into legal and accepted practices. In Colombia in 2002, for example, labour law reforms lengthened the working day, cut overtime pay premiums, reduced severance pay, and introduced more flexible contracts. In Indonesia, new legislation in 2003 normalised the previously unregulated use of short-term contracts. Research in 12 shoe, garment, and metal-goods factories in West Java found between 15 and 95 per cent of workers repeatedly hired on three- to twelve-month contracts, despite their employment in jobs not temporary or seasonal by nature. Likewise in the UK, a long-established loophole in the law allows home-based workers to be paid only 80 per cent of the national minimum wage (Oxfam International 2004).

Many governments are effectively creating a two-tier labour force within the formal economy. In the top tier, employers and the state take responsibility for covering the costs of maintaining a healthy workforce. Compensation ensures that workers are rested and ready for work (through paid leave time), receive a living wage for reasonable working hours, as well as time and expenses to stay healthy (through sick leave and health and accident coverage), and life-cycle needs such as maternity leave and pensions. In the bottom tier, by contrast, jobs are atomised, with employers limiting remuneration to 'production delivered' or 'time actually at work'. By not providing employment benefits, employers and the state are shirking their responsibilities for covering the real costs of creating a healthy, productive society — and women as carers are paying the price.

Defining the hidden costs of precarious employment

Precarious conditions of employment generate many hidden costs for women workers. We refer to these costs as 'hidden' for several reasons. Some are not explicitly recognised by workers to be costs, because they lack information about their rightful benefits under law, or because the costs materialise only in the longer term. Such costs are usually missing from official statistics of export-oriented employment produced by economists and policy makers. In addition, some costs are implicit subsidies of the true cost of production, because women workers are forced to pay out of their own pockets or forgo their rightful earnings.

In order to capture the full range of the hidden costs faced by workers in these sectors, we created a matrix (Figure 2) which brings together various contexts that determine the costs, and the different forms

of costs incurred. We developed this matrix towards the end of our research process and then understood the usefulness of such an analytical tool. We hope it may be of use or inspiration to other researchers and women's organisations addressing these issues.

We have defined four broad categories of 'contextual determinants'. First, *community relations*, such as networks providing child-care and credit, may be weakened when women have little time to participate. Likewise, women's social status may suffer from negative community perceptions: in Sri Lanka, for example, some marriage advertisements in newspapers say 'Garment women, please do not reply' (Oxfam International 2004, 28). Second, *household relations* that determine child-care roles and expectations may influence the redistribution of entitlements within a household once a woman takes on paid work. Male family members who formerly provided women with income support may withdraw it when women start to earn cash (Elson 1999). Third, *labour-law enforcement and compliance* determine, for example, access to maternity leave or health insurance. Employers are responsible for compliance with the law, but governments are ultimately responsible for the law's enforcement. The two interact closely and therefore in this framework they are combined. Lastly, *supply-chain pressures* of short production times, flexible and erratic orders, and low prices push many costs and risks of production on to managers, who pass them on to workers.

We have identified four forms of hidden costs for women workers that result from these contextual determinants. First, *out-of-pocket costs*: money paid out for goods and services required as a result of precarious terms of employment. Workers may expect to pay for bus fares to work or for lunch at work, but not for phone calls home or taxis late at night as a result of overtime at short notice. Likewise, workers may expect to pay for their rent when they migrate to find a job, but not for a doctor's visit when health contributions are deducted from their salaries. The second form of hidden costs is *income and benefits forgone*: rightful income and benefits not received, such as unpaid overtime or maternity leave. Third are *human development costs* in terms of ill-health due to poor working environment and inadequate time to spend with the family as a result of excessive overtime. Lastly are the costs to *equity and self-esteem* as a result of more unequal gender relations or intimidation in the workplace which undermine an individual's sense of self-worth.

The following quotes demonstrate the variety of hidden costs borne by women workers. The matrix provides a useful tool not only for documenting those already known, but for raising awareness about those that have not yet been identified.

Cost: out of pocket / Context: supply-chain pressures:

'We are often told on the same day that we have to work overtime that evening. It is then our responsibility to make arrangements with the [transport] services we use. We have to pay for the phone call…women who have children have to make special arrangements…We are not given adequate warning to come to work prepared' – Linkie, a South African fruit-packhouse worker (Smith et al. 2003).

Cost: out of pocket / Context: labour-law enforcement and compliance:

'We have asked for protective clothes, but they say it is too expensive for the farm and we should pay for the clothes' – Katryn, South African apple picker (Oxfam International 2004, 75).

Cost: income forgone / Context: supply-chain pressures:

Morocco garment workers put in around 90 hours of overtime in July 2003 under pressure to meet the buyer's tight deadline but the employer counted them not as overtime but as hours required to complete set targets. The women received only 50 to 60 per cent of their rightful pay as a result (Oxfam International 2004).

Cost: human development / Context: household relations:

In Morocco, of women garment workers with children old enough to care for siblings, 80 per cent had taken daughters under 14 out of school to care for younger siblings, sacrificing their education and future prospects (Oxfam International 2004).

Cost: self-esteem and equity / Context: labour-law enforcement and compliance:

'Supervisors abuse us…if we talk, they say, "Shut your beak! Even a child can do your job"' – Lucy, a Kenyan garment worker (Oxfam International 2004, 16).

Figure 2: Determinants and forms of hidden costs for women workers

| | | Contextual determinant of cost | | | |
		Supply- chain pressures	Labour-law enforcement and compliance	Household relations	Community relations
Form of hidden cost	Out of pocket				
	Income/benefit forgone				
	Human development				
	Self-esteem and equity				

Cost: self-esteem and equity / Context: community relations:

'As a woman you sacrifice your life, your health, your youth…you are downtown at a party, you are shopping and no matter how well dressed you are, you can smell the odour of sulphur and they point at you saying, "There goes a temporary worker, a grapevine worker"' – Anna, a grape picker in Chile (CEDEM 2003, 26).

Documenting the price of hidden costs

The campaign of Oxfam and its partners aims to highlight the impact on women workers of supply-chain pressures and governments' failure to protect labour rights. As a result, we focused on documenting the out-of-pocket costs and the income and benefits forgone specifically as a result of the emerging model of supply-chain flexibility and inadequate government protection. Below, four examples are given, from research conducted with garment workers in Bangladesh, tomato pickers in the United States, home-based workers in the United Kingdom, and garment workers in Honduras.

Bangladesh: forgone income costs of overtime

Women garment workers interviewed from seven factories in 2003 worked on average 80 hours of overtime per month. They knew that they were being underpaid for it, but not one received a written pay slip and so they were not aware of the extent of underpayment. Researchers at the Human Development Research Centre calculated the pay that they should have received with the premium due on overtime. The results showed that their actual pay was just 60–80 per cent of their due earnings, and the loss was equivalent to doing 24 hours of unpaid work per month. In addition, they faced out-of-pocket expenses: workers can walk home in daylight hours but had to pay transport costs late at night after overtime – costs that were equivalent to 17 hours of unpaid work in a month (Barkat et al. 2003, cited in Oxfam International 2004).

USA: forgone income costs of temporary contracts

In the United States, agricultural workers are excluded from many protections under national labour legislation and are often not covered by state law either. In Immokalee, Florida, three out of four tomato pickers are young Mexican men, many of them undocumented workers, hired on temporary contracts and paid on a piece-rate basis.

Researchers at Oxfam America calculated the value of income and benefits forgone as a result of not being employed as a long-term worker. They first calculated the saving to employers by comparing the cost of hiring a temporary employee with the cost of paying a long-term farm worker to do the same job.

At the height of the picking season, temporary workers work seven days a week, 11 hours a day – that is, 308 hours per month. The piece-rate is 45 cents per bucket, and the average worker can fill 100 buckets per day. The total monthly cost to an employer – and the total income of the worker – is, therefore, 45 cents for 100 buckets for 28 days, that is, $1,260.

A long-term employee, working 11 hours a day for 28 days, would qualify for 148 hours of overtime per month (paid at a premium) on top of a basic 40-hour working week, paid at the minimum wage. Long-term employees are also eligible for social security and unemployment insurance, towards which employers must pay a contribution. Table 1 shows the total cost.

Table 1: Costs of hiring a full-time farm worker in Florida, USA

Wages and benefits	Calculation	US $
Minimum wage	5.15/hour x 160	824
Overtime pay	1.5 x 5.15 x 148	1143
Social security tax	7.65% x (wages + overtime)	150
Unemployment insurance tax	6.2% x (wages + overtime)	122
TOTAL		2239

For the employer, then, the saving is $979 per month, or 44 per cent of a stable employee's costs. For employers, this is efficient cost saving which can then be turned into more competitive wholesale prices.

For workers, though, the hidden costs are substantial. The research covered only the income forgone as a result of being paid piece-rate: $707 per month. Additional research could include creating data on the frequency of required health visits and the cost of treatment, additional transport or childcare costs because of the hours of work involved, and the value of unemployment insurance for families. Likewise, human-development costs of long hours could be estimated: how many hours fewer would workers choose to put in, given that, as a full-time employees, they could earn the equivalent of their current gross wages in 217 hours, rather than 308 hours, per month? (Oxfam International 2004).

UK: forgone income costs of being a home-based worker

In the UK, manufacturers provide home workers with assembly kits (for making Christmas crackers, for example) that they say will take 14 hours to complete. Home workers are required to sign an agreement to this effect, but report that the kits actually take 40 hours to complete. In addition, UK law has long permitted employers to pay homeworkers only 80 per cent of the national minimum wage.[3] Researchers at the National Group on Home Working estimated the savings to employers and the income forgone to workers due to these policies and practices.

For employers, the cost of a factory-based worker for an eight-hour day is the national minimum wage of £4.50 per hour, plus contribution to national insurance and holiday costs of £3.91, creating a total of £39.91 per day. A home-based worker doing the same work on the actual piece-rate pay described above, and without any requisite benefit contributions, costs the employer only £11.00 per eight-hour day. Hence the employer saves £28.91 per day. The income forgone by workers due to piece-rate pay on the unrealistic time basis is £25 per day. Further research could calculate the value to the individual of the benefits forgone, through data on the value of unemployment benefits and the number of days of paid leave permitted under employment law (Oxfam International 2004).

Honduras: the threat of forgone income and benefits for garment workers

In Honduras the government is currently proposing a new 'temporary work law' which would permit garment factories to hire up to 30 per cent of their workers on temporary, instead of permanent, contracts – driven by the desire to provide the kind of flexible and low-cost labour force that foreign and local investors are seeking. Researchers at the Honduran Alliance for Labour Protection have estimated that, if the law is passed, the industry's employers could switch one worker in three on to such a contract, saving a total of US$90m over three years. For workers, that would mean forgoing the income and benefits of paid leave, social security, and an annual bonus, a figure which could be calculated in monetary terms with further research (Oxfam International 2004).

Conclusion: opportunities for further analysis

The matrix and calculations of hidden costs presented above are intended to help to capture the broader consequences of precarious employment for workers in global supply chains. It could be taken forward in several ways.

First, further research could ascribe monetary values to benefits forgone and out-of-pocket expenses, through detailed surveys of the needs and spending patterns of the workers concerned. Second, the matrix could be completed in depth for a particular set of women workers during a focus-group discussion. Identifying and documenting hidden costs in this way could help to raise awareness among those workers of their rights at work and would provide data useful for campaigning. Third, such information could be used by worker organisers to identify which of the hidden costs they can most immediately reduce or eliminate – by demanding, for example, a free phone call each when required to do overtime at short notice. Though this would be a small initial step, it would help to shift the assumptions about who should pay for flexible production. Lastly, the matrix could be extended to include hidden long-term costs to society – for example, by estimating the future public-health costs of failing to enforce laws on health and safety at work today, or by estimating the government revenue forgone – and the health care or education it could have paid for – by providing tax holidays to foreign investors today.

Identifying and documenting hidden costs in the ways suggested above helps to clarify what is at stake when retailers offload costs and risks down their supply chains and when governments, keen to meet their demands, fail to enforce the law or, worse still, weaken it. It shows exactly who is paying – literally subsidising – production costs in the name of supply chain efficiencies and flexible labour markets. It demonstrates how women – as workers and carers – are paying the price of governments' trade and investment strategies that rely on precarious jobs, with negative consequences for gender equality. We hope that it will also contribute in some way to start reversing this unjust trend.

Kate Raworth is a researcher and policy adviser at Oxfam GB. She is the author of Trading Away our Rights: Women Working in Global Supply Chains *(Oxfam International 2004).*
kraworth@oxgam.org.uk

Thalia Kidder is Oxfam GB's global adviser on Labour and Gendered Economics. She has worked for trade union networks and women's economic development in North and Central America.
tkidder@oxfam.org.uk

Notes

1 Thanks to Mary Sue Smiaroski for helpful comments on an earlier draft.
2 Trade unions have also done considerable work for and with workers in precarious employment. Women are the great majority of these workers, and therefore women workers' organisations have often been at the forefront of these struggles.
3 At the time of writing, this loophole in UK law was due to be closed by the autumn of 2004.

References

CEDEM (2003) 'Consequences and Costs of Precarious Employment for Women Workers in the Chilean Agro-Exports Sector', Santiago: Oxfam GB and Oxfam Canada.

Dolan, C. and K. Sorby (2003) 'Gender and Employment in High-value Agriculture and Rural Industries', Agricultural and Rural Development Working Paper Series No. 7, Washington DC: World Bank.

Elson, D. (1999) 'Labour Markets as Gender Institutions: Equality, Efficiency and Empowerment Issues', *World Development*, 27(3): 611–627.

Krugman, P. (1997) 'In Praise of Cheap Labour', http://web.mit.edu/krugman/www/smokey.html (last checked by the authors March 2004).

Oxfam International (2004) *Trading Away Our Rights: Women working in Global Supply Chains*, Oxford: Oxfam GB, www.maketradefair.com (last checked by the authors March 2004).

Smith, S., D. Auret, S. Barrientos, C. Dolan, K. Kleinbooi, C. Njovu, M. Opondo and A. Tallontire (2003) 'Ethical Trade in African Horticulture: Gender, Rights and Participation', preliminary report presented at a multi-stakeholder workshop, Institute of Development Studies, 26 June 2003.

Global trade and home work:

closing the divide

Annie Delaney

Home work has re-emerged as a new form of subcontracted production. Promoted through global capital, it relies on sweatshop labour conditions to cut costs and maintain workers in a vulnerable state. There are now an estimated 300 million home workers in the global workforce, who are part of the growing informal employment sector. In many instances, they are denied a living wage, safe working conditions, basic decent living standards, and recognition as workers. They can be found in every country, are mostly women, and are usually invisible. These women are slowly being recognised as the most marginalised and disadvantaged workers, as their numbers increase and the work system is extended to other industry sectors.

Since the 1970s the Japanese system of 'just-in-time' production, demanding rapid turn-around time for suppliers, has become the model for many companies. Toyota, for example, uses an estimated 38,000 sub-contractors, using many small workshops which rely on home workers. Home workers produce goods for companies subcontracted by big brand names, such as Phillips in the Netherlands or Siemens in Northern Greece.[1]

In addition to work in subcontracting companies, 'own-account' or independent home workers in remote, rural locations are increasingly linked into global markets. Handicraft production in India such as Kutch embroidery, for example, is a growing export sector; as a general trend, the quality of the embroidery has declined as exports, prices, and popularity have increased, driving prices down. As handicraft work becomes more commercialised, workers become more dependent, and pay and conditions usually deteriorate.

Trade is not free: women pay the cost

'I have worked knitting and packing cards for 10 years. Lately, I have also been assembling circuit boards for televisions and other electrical goods. I work much harder than workers in the factory, but I get paid less, and it is hard to think that things will improve.' (Jean, home worker in the UK)

A measurable effect of trade liberalisation is declining working conditions, which contribute to the expansion and growth of the informal workforce. Fierce competition by governments to gain or maintain producer-country status in the export sector exacerbates this trend. Where they exist, laws to protect workers' rights are often unofficially rewritten to remove employers' core obligations such as allowing workers the right to organise, and freedom of association.[2]

Home workers fall into two categories: dependent workers who are paid piece rates and usually produce for a subcontractor, or intermediary companies in a contract chain. In addition, independent or 'own-account' workers produce goods for direct sale through street stalls, shops, or the local village. They themselves determine what products they make and where they sell them.

The informal economy is rapidly expanding in every country. It includes the contract labour of factories and call centres, street vendors, domestic workers, rag pickers, migrant workers, construction and forest workers, and produce harvesters, as well as home workers. The global informal employment sector is huge and largely consists of female, unprotected workers. In many countries the only new employment creation is in the informal, unorganised sector. As part of this trend, home work is increasingly used in industries such as garments, shoes, metal works and car manufacturing, jewellery and gems, food preparation and selling, packing and assembly of fresh and manufactured goods, and a broad range of services.

Despite this, home workers are rarely mentioned in national statistics, or recognised as part of the workforce, or acknowledged in the national economy. Most governments are content to keep the informal sector undefined and vague. Further, home workers are often neglected in the strategies of unions and non-government agencies, which tend to focus on income-generation schemes without making the links to working conditions and the need to organise for general improvements. Employers largely benefit from a large pool of invisible, underpaid, and isolated workers.

The garment industry provides a good example of the deteriorating conditions that workers face, although the major brands are often quick to deny that home workers are present in their supply chain. Recently, grassroots organisations in Asia and Eastern Europe, supported by 'Working Women Worldwide', conducted research on subcontracting in the garment industry.[3] They found evidence of home working in every country involved in the study. All the international subcontracting chains involved home workers, producing goods for major brands in Europe, the USA, and Japan.

Few of the international voluntary codes mention home work; if they do, there is no process for ensuring that the codes will be monitored and made relevant to home workers. The International Labour Organization (ILO) passed Convention 177 on Homebased Work in 1996.[4] It has been ratified by four countries: Ireland, Finland, Netherlands, and Albania, although in these countries the impact has been poorly documented. We know that a substantial amount of home work is done in Albania, for example, as Italian firms subcontract foot-wear work there. However, despite the existence of the code, there are few unions or organisations working with Albanian home workers, and much work is needed to push for the implementation of the Convention.

There are some countries where campaigns and organising have proven to be effective strategies for improving home workers' conditions. For instance, in India a number of groups, including Adithi, Women's Forum, and SEWA, are lobbying for recognition, protection, and a policy on home work and a 'National Act for Workers in Informal Employment'.

In Australia, the government has refused to ratify the Homeworkers' Convention, but state laws have been introduced to protect home workers. Campaigns to ratify the Convention often increase visibility, recognition, and the potential to improve national protection of home workers.

In other countries, attempts to organise have not been so successful. The experience of workers in Export Processing Zones (EPZs) in Baguio, The Philippines, demonstrates increasing similarities between conditions for factory workers on temporary contracts (or operating as subcontracted labour) and home workers. Garment-factory employers in this area rely on subcontracting to small workshops and home workers. They utilise contacts in factories to distribute work to others outside the factory. The factory worker has become the link from the factory to the home workers. Attempts by workers in the Baguio region to form unions have resulted in the relocation of whole factories to other regions and the loss of jobs, despite the fact that the brands involved have a Code of Conduct which provides the right to organise and freedom of association. The Gap is one the largest buyers of clothing from The Philippines. Manufacturers producing Gap and other major brand garments use factory relocation as a strategy to reduce labour costs, discourage worker organisation, and increase profit. Moving to the Southern Luzon region can reduce the hourly rate paid to workers from US $5.60 to $4.70 and, for workers on short-term contracts, to $3.50 an hour (Reyes, 2003).

Movement between permanent work, monthly contract work, seasonal work, and the lowest-paid home work increases the precarious situation for workers. The flexibility demanded under the current terms of international trade forces workers to reshape how they earn money to survive. Homebased work in the garment industry in The Philippines accounts for more than one third of production in the EPZs. The redefinition of a worker's relationship with the factory is a critical aspect of efforts to attract and retain foreign customers. The easier it is to sack workers or to shift them to less stable, more flexible, and lower-paid work arrangements, the more reassured the buyer will usually be that the workers won't cause any problems(Torafing, 2003).

This is a critical time for workers in informal sectors to improve their capacity to organise collectively. Otherwise global trade regimes will lead to reduced standards for all workers.

New ways to organise home-based workers

Globally a number of groups have supported the development of new home-worker organisations. Homeworkers Worldwide (HWW) is one of the groups that have emerged to support grassroots organising and to document models for organising home-based workers. HWW has co-ordinated a programme to develop and link activities into existing and new unions and home-worker organisations.[5]

HWW has documented one example from Australia to demonstrate how a union began to organise homebased workers. The Textile, Clothing and Footwear Union of Australia (TCFUA), and the community campaign, 'FairWear' have used information on subcontracted chains to improve home workers' conditions, organise home workers, achieve legislation, and put in place a retailers'/manufacturers' code specific to home workers.

Targeting the public

Ten years ago no one in Australia really knew much about home workers, but today if you ask a person on the street you will probably be told that they are likely to be women sewing clothes in sweatshop conditions. Brands and retailers are sensitive to this level of consumer awareness. The campaign used the simple comparison between a home worker's wage of $2.00 to make a garment and the retail price of $150.00 for the same garment. Consumers were lobbied to support fair wages for home workers and to urge their favourite brands to engage in ethical practices.

Community campaigning by FairWear mobilised consumers by using direct action outside storefronts and corporate headquarters to publicly shame retailers into taking responsibility for the conditions of home workers producing their goods. Visual, creative, and media-friendly stunts increased home workers' visibility and recognition by pressuring retailers to sign the Homeworkers' Code, and linking this to government policies and workers' need for legal protection.

Targeting the government

The campaign aimed for legislative reform at state and federal levels to improve home workers' protection and rights as workers.

A 1995 TCFUA report,[6] documenting the conditions of home workers, contributed to a Australian Senate inquiry; subsequent media exposure forced the industry to respond formally to the problems identified. To date, legislation giving home workers in the garment industry legal status as employees has been implemented in five states.

The national Senate inquiry into home work in the garment industry in 1996 led to the introduction of the Voluntary Homeworkers' Code of Practice, after employers were forced to sit down with the union and come up with some solutions. A pay-equity inquiry in the state of New South Wales led to improved legal protection for garment home workers. In other states, similar legislation has been passed in response to inquiries, research, and campaigning. In May 2003 in Victoria, legislation was passed to give home workers recognition as workers, the right to claim unpaid remuneration from the retailer or brand, and a process to review the Voluntary Retailers' Code, with the potential for it to become mandatory.

FairWear opposed initiatives to reduce workers' protection in national labour laws, pointing out the potential impact on already disadvantaged home workers. The federal government is committed to further deregulation and decreased worker protection, and so the campaign has kept the spotlight on the impact on the most vulnerable workers.

Using the law and codes

The Australian national industry law known as the 'Clothing Trades Award'

aims to ensure that home-based workers and other workers receive their legal entitlements. Home workers earn on average \$2–\$3 (US\$1–\$1.50) an hour, compared with the legal minimum rate of \$13 (US\$7.50) an hour. The union began to prosecute large groups of companies for breaches of this Award. In one state, more than 100 companies were prosecuted in a five-year period between 1998 and 2003, for more than 800 breaches.

Using negative publicity, FairWear encouraged a group of companies that were being prosecuted to sign the Code. One event involved protesters, wearing nothing but their underwear, shouting 'We would rather wear nothing than be clothed in exploitation.' Customers abandoned the targeted store for days following this protest, and the company did eventually sign the Code. In the same period, a group of home workers came forward to take the first claims against companies for their legal entitlements; ultimately they agreed to out-of-court settlements. And in 2003 Nike signed the Sportswear and Corporate-wear section of the Code.[7] The campaign's effectiveness stemmed from the fact that home workers became more visible, but avoided identifying themselves, because of the risk of reprisals or loss of work.

Targeting home workers

The organising of Australian home workers began through training, advocacy, and multilingual communication. Over time, home workers provided information about company practice, spoke to the media and at union rallies, participated in research and video projects, and allowed federal and state politicians to visit their houses to see at first hand how they worked. Confidence and trust building were important elements in workers' participation.

At FairWear, we brought groups of home workers together to document their problems, discuss what could be done, and examine where they were placed in the contract chain. We recorded the labels that they worked for and linked these brands directly to poor working conditions, low wages, harassment and abuse, child labour, and health-related issues. One group of home workers formed a lobbying and education group to campaign for legislation. They were trained to speak to the media, politicians and community leaders. The home workers protested outside politicians' offices, shared their personal stories with supporters and media, and met with other home workers. Vietnamese-speaking home workers, a majority group, began their own radio programme, called *Outworkers' voice*, reaching thousands of home workers. Home-worker leadership has developed through these interlinked activities.

Australian Homeworkers' Code

The Australian labour law provides home workers in the garment sector pay equity with factory workers. However, this rarely applies. The majority are from refugee and migrant communities, unaware of their rights, or too frightened to make a complaint in case they lose their work. Employers and subcontractors could and would dispute their claims, as the home workers speak little English, rarely have written documentation, and are considered contractors with no rights.

Companies applying to become accredited to the Homeworkers' Code must demonstrate that they have systems in place to guarantee that any home workers producing clothes for their subcontractors are employed under (at least) minimum wages and conditions. They must provide to the joint 'Union–Employer Code Committee' details of their suppliers, and include evidence that their suppliers are meeting legal conditions. They must provide examples of work records, including a calculated piece rate based on hourly pay rates. When a company gains accreditation status, it is

given permission to attach a label reading 'No Sweatshop' to its garments as a sign of compliance and is promoted as a 'good guy' by the campaign.[8]

Companies' information on their supply chains enables the unions to follow suppliers and to build up an information base about where the work is going in the industry.

Home workers making products for companies accredited to the Voluntary Homeworkers' Code are, for the first time, receiving workers' compensation insurance, superannuation (pension) payments, and increased pay rates. Following recent prosecutions, about 30 companies are seeking accreditation, which is a significant improvement on the four accredited since 2001.

Experiences elsewhere

HWW is currently completing a three-year mapping project, supported by Department for International Development (DFID) in the UK. HWW set out to document models and strategies for organising homebased workers, using action research. More than 30 country and regional groups linked to the project have begun to identify where home workers are located, and the industries in which they work. The second step involves the formation of organisations and unions. The project has already facilitated new home-worker groups in Eastern Europe, China, Indonesia, and Latin America.

The mapping has two aspects. The first – horizontal mapping – documents the location of home workers and the nature of the work. It is common for home workers to be trained as part of the action research team, a fact which assists in building the organisation.

The second aspect of the project – vertical mapping – is a process which traces or 'maps' the local, national, and international subcontracting chains, with the aim of strengthening the home-based workers' position and ultimately helping to improve their working and living conditions.[9]

There are numerous examples of positive outcomes through this project.[10] For instance, in the southern state of Tamil Nadu, India, a local rural organisation, READ Foundation, has been working with the mapping programme to set up self-help groups with home-based garment workers. These groups were initially savings groups but gradually they have taken up other activities, helping women to buy raw materials in bulk and sell their products collectively. READ has worked with and been supported by the local union to train home workers and lobby for better conditions. Workers have secured improved wages and some legal protection by using the union's knowledge of existing legislation. The READ Foundation has helped home workers to join the Tamil Nadu Manual Workers' Board , which secures benefits for workers. READ is now organising garment home workers into unions and applying a similar strategy to groups of home workers in other industries.

In Chile, as part of the mapping programme, home workers in the seaweed business in the south, supported by the women's organisation, Centre for Training for Women Workers (CECAM), organised to improve living conditions by removing the middlemen from the supply chain. Workers received training and support from CECAM to organise and develop a group. Their incomes have more than doubled, and they now have greater control over how they work, without pressure from the middlemen. They are part of an international contracting chain, selling seaweed to international cosmetic and food producers.

Home-worker support groups such as READ in Tamil Nadu and CECAM in Chile have developed strong alliances with local unions to encourage home workers to organise. These alliances build on the skills of local organisations and trade unions to help home workers to form their own unions or join existing ones, in order to improve their legal status and living standards.

In Chile, CECAM is encouraging the formation of local organisations of home workers in the garment and footwear sectors, through education and support. These new groups have formed regional organisations and are developing alliances with formal trade unions. Some factories and workshops in the chains have been identified, and the formal unions in the factories have been contacted. We can see in this a potentially powerful alliance between formal and informal worker organisations.

Conclusion

The threat of losing work is very real and is often used by corporations. Home workers face many obstacles and are certainly more vulnerable if they draw attention to brand-name labour practices. This article has demonstrated the importance of incorporating home workers into training and organising strategies in sensitive ways, and of bringing together formal and informal workers.

Increasing demands for flexibility from buyer-driven chains push prices down and place unreasonable demands on suppliers. As consumers, we need to ask the brand owners some hard questions. But the solution does not lie solely with consumers in industrialised countries. Alliance building across organisations, increased community awareness about workers' conditions and rights, and support for worker organisations at the grassroots level are strategies which have been proven to work. Workers and their organisations can make trade work by ensuring that corporations play by fair rules.

Annie Delaney has worked as a community campaigner for more than 20 years, most recently as an active participant in the FairWear campaign and working for the Textile, Clothing and Footwear Union of Australia in support of home workers. Annie has been involved in HomeNet International and is on the international advisory committee of Homeworkers Worldwide. She is currently

working on a campaigning manual for home-worker groups.
Contact adelaney@melbpc.org.au

Notes

1 European Homeworkers' Group (1998) 'Report on Homework in European Subcontracting Chains'.

2 It is common in Export Processing Zones that unofficial No Union–No Strike policies are administered to reduce legal protection for workers. For example, in areas of The Philippines, Indonesia and Mexico the government support for implementation of such unofficial policies is acted out through military suppression of workers, abuse of union leaders, and support for government-backed non-democratic unions.

3 Women Working Worldwide, 'Subcontracting in the Garment Industry', Women Working Worldwide Project Workshop, Bangkok, February 2003. See www.women-ww.org or infor@women-ww.org for more information.

4 ILO Homework Convention No.177 and its recommendations, if ratified, requires governments to develop national policy around the issues for home-based workers and asserts the principal of equal remuneration for home-based workers as for enterprise-based workforce.

5 HomeNet as an international network was formally dissolved in 2003, but a number of network members are part of Homeworkers Worldwide and other informal networks.

6 Textile, Clothing and Footwear Union of Australia (1995) 'The Hidden Cost of Fashion', Sydney.

7 Homeworkers' Code of Practice Committee, HomeWorkers' Code of Practice (1996), Sports and Corporate Wear Ethical Clothing Deed, (2003). See www.nosweatshoplabel.com re: Homeworkers' Code of Practice.

8 FairWear wallet card is a guide for consumers on where to shop and not to shop. www.fairwear.org.com or fairwear@vic.uca.org.au.

9 Homeworkers Worldwide horizontal and vertical mapping packs, 2003. Contact: www.homeworksww.org.uk or mapping@homeworksww.org.uk for more information.

10 Examples from Chile and India are drawn from *Campaigns at Work: A Guide to Campaigning for Homebased Worker Organisations, Unions, Campaign Groups and Activists* by Annie Delaney (HomeWorkers Worldwide UK, 2004).

References

Reyes, Diane (2003) 'The Production and Distribution Structure of the International Garment and Textile Subcontracting Chain', Philippine Resource Centre, Manila.

Torafing, Christina (2003) 'Research on the Subcontracting Chain in the Garment Industry', Innabuyog Metro-Baguio, The Philippines.

Women workers and precarious employment in Shenzhen Special Economic Zone, China

Pun Ngai

In spite of the increase in transnational codes of conduct and legal mobilisation of labour, despotic labour regimes in China are still prevalent. Globalisation and 'race to the bottom' production strategies adopted by transnational corporations militate against the improvement of labour relations in China. The goal of this study is to provide a framework for understanding the working conditions of female migrant workers. While the inhumane working conditions of the women workers have been repeatedly observed, none of the existing studies has provided a solid analysis of the precarious employment system in China. This article aims to span global factors as well as local elements, demonstrating how they each contribute to precarious employment patterns. The hidden costs of the production and reproduction cycles are still unknown.[1]

As China has become increasingly incorporated into the global economy over the past two decades, it has developed into a 'world workshop', providing a huge pool of cheap labour for global production. Since the mid-1990s we have witnessed a surge in the relocation of transnational corporations in China, especially from Hong Kong, Taiwan, Japan, the USA, and Western Europe. More than 100 million peasant workers work in transnational corporations which are directly owned or joint-ventured by American and European companies, or they work for Chinese companies which act as contractors and subcontractors for these companies. There are concerns emerging among NGOs as well as in academic circles about globalisation and labour conditions in post-socialist China.

The 'Chinese Working Women Network' (CWWN) started its project in the Special Economic Zone (SEZ) in Shenzhen, just across the border from Hong Kong. Since 1996 we have witnessed the rapid incorporation of migrant labourers in this SEZ, which was set up in 1980. Before this, Shenzhen was only a small city with 310,000 residents and fewer than 30,000 workers. At the end of the year 2000, the total population had increased to 4.33 million, and its labour force to 3.09 million. Around 30 per cent of the population are categorised as permanent residents who have come from major cities as state officials, entrepreneurs, technicians, and skilled workers. About 70 per cent are classed as temporary residents, a status which means that they do not have the official household registration entitling them to citizenship in Shenzhen. In 2000, the total number of temporary residents was 3.08 million, which constitutes almost the entire labour force in Shenzhen, the majority being migrant labourers from rural areas.

The rapid economic development of Shenzhen and the advancement of its position in the global economy is dependent on the extraction of female labour from the rural areas. The process of 'globalising' Shenzhen has depended on cheap and 'compliant' female labour, in the development of export-processing industries. In our studies in garment and electronics plants in Shenzhen, we found that more than 90 per cent of the total labour force in the light manufacturing industries was young, female, and under 25 years of age. All women workers were classified as rural peasant workers, or *mingong*. No matter how long they had worked in Shenzhen, they could never be classified as formal workers. Lacking the right to stay in the city, most were accommodated in the workers' dormitories provided by their employers.

Migrant workers and the dormitory labour regime

The 'dormitory labour regime' in China contributes to an exploitative employment system. This regime links with labour migration and reproduction cycles in the rural communities, serves global production, and generates hidden costs which are borne by women workers. Local governments compete for foreign investment, openly neglecting legal regulations and social provisions. The costs of labour reproduction, such as education and general welfare, are entirely undertaken by the rural communities which subsidise wages, accommodation and consumption. Wages of migrant workers are equal to those of ten years ago, or are declining, but the lack of residential status in the city precludes the formation of a working-class force which could work for the labour rights of migrant workers.

The shrinking of the government role in labour provisions has resulted in a lack of social and labour protections for rural migrant workers. Deprived of their rights to stay in the city, there is almost no long-term planning for education, training, housing, medical care, and social welfare to accommodate the new working class. As half-peasants, half-workers, migrant labourers have ambiguous citizenship rights and weak

bargaining power. They are forced to leave the city if they lose their job, no matter how long they have been working there.

Without state protections, female migrant workers resort to the support of familial networks. These networks facilitate migration flows and job searches, circulate work information, and help workers cope with factory life and hardship in the city. Most of the invisible costs assumed by familial networks have the effect of benefiting industry. Such costs include labour recruitment, training, and discipline. Reliant on labour networks to train workers, and to assist with their adjustment to factory life, management continues to maximise profit and promote the precarious employment system in China.

In order to illustrate how the precarious employment system arises in China we will look at labour use, including working conditions, migration and reproduction cycles. We will show that the patriarchal culture in rural China that affects the migration process and reproduction of labour also shapes the labour conditions in special economic zones. Our research covers five factories where CWWN has assisted in long-term organising in the workers' dormitories since 2000. We conducted organising activities as well as research with more than 1,500 women workers in these garment factories.

Women, family, and reproduction

It is often stressed that the low status of Chinese women is rooted in the Chinese family system, which is patrilineal, patrilocal, and patriarchal in nature. Women in rural China were traditionally deprived of the means of production and the right to land, and their personal autonomy was totally submerged under male authority. They were temporary members of their natal families, and strangers/intruders in their husbands' families (Johnson, 1983). Women were born into a system where they were essentially powerless. Their labour would be given to another family, and they were therefore considered as 'water spilled on the ground', as one Chinese saying goes. No family would invest time and money in educating daughters who one day would become the daughter-in-law of someone else.

Forty years' experience of socialism in China did not fulfill its promise of 'women's liberation', which was one of the significant revolutionary goals. The priorities of economic and political development overshadowed the goals of social change, sacrificing women's emancipation.

Socialism and patriarchy have to date existed together in harmonious stability. The configuration of a patrilocal/patrilineal/patriarchal family system has been even further consolidated in the reform period of recent years. When land was restored to the household, when the male household-head represented all female interests, women's rights and situation further deteriorated (Croll, 1985). Worse still, the government's one-child policy controls not only women's fertility, but also their bodies, sexuality, and personal autonomy. Consequently neither socialist revolution nor reformist transformation created more opportunity for women to expand their horizons.

Most of the factory women whom we interviewed knew quite well before they left their villages that they were going to be imprisoned in sweatshops for twelve hours each day, earning about five or six hundred *renminbi* (US$60-72) each month. The youngest woman in the workplaces was 16, and the oldest was 46; they all knew that the factory boss would not treat them as equal human beings. They knew there was a huge gap between industrial life and rural life. They knew they were going to sell their bodies. They knew almost everything.

Dong: 'It's not the first time I've gone out working'

Dong was a rural female migrant worker typical of her generation. At the age of 23, she was an experienced *dagongmei* (working daughter) and had been working in Guangdong for more than four years. Dong was born in a relatively poor village in Hunan. She grew up along with China's rapid economic reform over the past 20 years. As the eldest daughter, her father asked her to quit her junior secondary school at the age of 16, when her younger brother entered secondary school.

'I thought I could earn more money in the Special Economic Zone. I knew quite well what the working conditions might be, and how much I could earn before I went out to work. I knew it was not easy to work in a big city which was a totally strange place to me. But I thought it was still worth it to try, and it was a chance for me to look at the outside world.'

She went back home almost every year. Every time she returned, she brought back about two thousand yuan ($240) to her father, which was more than the total of her family's income. The family was happy with her contribution, and she was satisfied too. *'The first time I saw my father and mother smile so happily, I knew that there is big gap between urban life and rural life. My parents at first could not believe that I earned two thousand yuan within five months.'*

But for Dong, the life of the outside world became less and less interesting as she worked in Shenzhen for four years. *'I do feel tired. The working hours are too long. It's too hard. What's worse, I could never have hoped to stay in the city. My hukou (household registration) is in the village.[2] Last New Year, I went back home and thought that I would not come out again. I stayed home for two months and I slept, slept all the day.'* But with her energy and health restored, she felt bored at home and went out working again. She had a boyfriend living in a nearby village, and they agreed to get married the next year.

303090

She knew that after marriage she might have no chance to work in the city again. So, even though industrial work was very arduous and exploitative, she still wanted to enjoy her personal 'freedom' outside the village for a little more time. Saving some of the money for her future married life was another consideration. '*Life will be happy if my husband and my parents-in-law treat me nice. But no one knows. It's better for me to have some money of my own.*'

Thus the individual life cycle, the women's transitional life period between puberty and marriage, has meshed with social time, the transitional period of the socialist economy fusing with global capitalism.

Uprooting labour rights

Besides labour control, population control is another of China's strategies to recruit labour. Population control in China is affected by a system called *hukou*, household registration, which was formally set up in 1958. The *hukou* system in China determined not just where a person could live, but also the person's entire life chances - social rank, wage, welfare, food rations, and housing (Solinger, 1991). In the pre-Reform era, there was only one strict system of *hukou*: the registered urban permanent residence and rural permanent residence. Peasants, with their fate sealed by the rural *hukou*, were banned from leaving the land for more than three decades. Loopholes did exist, but in terms of numbers, illegal migration was never able to challenge the social order that was polarized between the rural peasantry and the urban working class.

Shenzhen was the first city to change its hukou system dramatically in the early 1980s. Besides the former permanent household registration, temporary household registration has been issued to temporary labourers. In Shenzhen the hukou system is well connected with labour control. Rural

migrants are hired by enterprises and approved as temporary labourers, after the payment of Increased City Capacity Fee. Enterprises should then apply to the Public Security Bureau for a certificate of temporary residence registration, and to the police station for a temporary *hukou* registration. And, finally, they should apply to the District Public Security Bureau for a Temporary Residence Certificate, so that their workers can become legal temporary workers in Shenzhen. The temporary residence is for one year only: it needs to be renewed annually, for a fee. The strategy of local governments is to change rural labour regularly. Local officials openly declared that if there was work, rural labour could be given a temporary residence. However, if there was no work, they would have to leave, so the local government would not have to bear the burdens of urbanisation.

The *houkou* system's distinction between permanent and temporary residents allows the state to shirk its obligation to provide housing, job security, and welfare to rural migrant workers. The labour of the rural population is needed, but once their labour ceases to be necessary they can no longer survive in the city. This newly forming working class is not permitted to form roots in the city. The *hukou* system, mixed with labour control, has created a deformed citizenship, which has disadvantaged Chinese migrants attempting to transform themselves into urban workers. The term *mingong*, 'peasant-workers' or temporary workers, blurs the lines of identity between peasant and worker (Solinger, 1999).

Housing, education, and other infrastructural services are not provided by the Shenzhen Government to the temporary residents. Migrant workers themselves are not rightful citizens and, moreover, their family members are not allowed to live in Shenzhen unless they too can find a job and acquire the status of temporary worker. Marriage and childbirth cannot be registered in Shenzhen. Officially these workers are still regarded as peasants and are supposed to have support from their families in the rural areas. The cost of labour reproduction is entirely borne by the rural society.

Normally a worker, usually female, will spend three to five years working as a wage labourer in an industrial city before getting married. The long-term planning of life activities such as marriage, procreation, and family are all expected in rural communities. Given that there is a great labour surplus in rural China, it is almost unnecessary for the urban government to consider the long-term reproduction of labour.

Most workers in Shenzhen live in factory dormitory buildings, with about 50 workers accommodated in one flat or house built of wood and iron sheet, provided by their employers. However, since the temporary labourers are not officially recognised as workers, or *gongren*, the factories do not recognise them as such either. One company director said that the workers whom they previously employed in Hong Kong were still under the protection of the labour law in Hong Kong, and they could not dismiss the workers arbitrarily without compensation. In Shenzhen, however, they could dismiss workers at any time they wanted to.

Working conditions

The notorious working conditions in the special economic zones and industrial towns in China can be attributed to the 'dormitory labour regime'. With accommodation tied to employment, the employer has control over the non-working life of the worker. With extended working, the employer can make it virtually impossible for workers to search for alternative employment. And the dormitory labour regime relies on young workers who can be easily controlled (Smith and Pun, 2003).

Dormitories are predominantly owned by local authorities and rented to factory owners. Increasingly however, foreign-invested firms are building their own dorms to suit their own particular needs; typically, these facilities are within compounds flanking the factory. In these settings, the spatial integration between working and non-working life is tighter, and companies, rather than the state, play a more commanding role in controlling workers' lives.

China Wonder Garments is a relatively small subcontracting garment factory set up in Shenzhen in 1989. China Wonder moved to Shenzhen from Hong Kong, attracted by lower production costs, cheaper land and labour, and the fact that the local state provided a better investment contract package, including lower taxes, management fees, and rents for a larger factory compound.

China Wonder has a workforce of 600, and is under a Hong Kong director who has sole authority over the operation and management of the factory, with a quasi-paternalistic style of management. It is situated in the middle of the global subcontracting chain, producing garments for Hong Kong buyers, who take their production orders from American and European corporations.

At the time of our research, both production and dormitory premises were rented from the local district government, which charged the company an additional management fee. Both production facilities and working environment were relatively poor, but there was no strong incentive to upgrade. The management knew that there was international pressure to improve the working and living conditions through codes of conduct. The Director had subscribed to the Disney Code of Conduct (a set of company codes on labour standards used to regulate subcontractors or suppliers in China since the mid 1990s), which was displayed on the wall in Chinese. He said that as these codes only gave verbal advice and no resources, they were not considered particularly helpful. Moreover, while a benchmark for the owner, they were also said to be 'window dressing'. It was stressed that profit margins were so tight, there was no room for additional costs.

Nearly all the workforce in China Wonder were rural migrant workers from the provinces of Guangdong, Hunan, Hubei, Jiangxi, Anhui, and Sichuan. The only locals of Shenzhen were the accountant and the housekeeper of the company. Housing these migrant workers was difficult and expensive, according to the housekeeper, though only very basic housing facilities were provided. The dormitory building, of three storeys, was just adjacent to the production building, which required only a two-minute walk to the shop floor, thus easily facilitating a 'just-in-time' labour system. Each dormitory room housed 12-16 workers and was very crowded, lacked ventilation or adequate lighting, and provided absolutely no private or individual space. Workers on each floor shared communal toilets and bathrooms at the end of the corridor. The management admitted that the living conditions were very poor, but blamed the local government for not providing enough space for adequate dormitory facilities. The dormitory building was built to accommodate 500 workers only, but it always had more than 600 workers.

The dorms provided by China Wonder were 'free', and no deposit for accommodation was required. A hierarchy for the spatial arrangement in lodging reinforced a hierarchy of labour. Managerial, technical, and supervisory staff members were sharing two per room, although these rooms were also very basic. Neo-paternalism in this workplace was reflected in the managerial style, as well as in the company reliance on family networks for recruitment. As an example, a supervisor in charge of 60 workers in the finishing unit had 12 relatives in the factory, and he had been with the company for six years. With 600 workers in the factory, it needed only about 50 families to be responsible for all recruitment. Access to the factory was therefore totally network-dependent, and strangers could not get in. Within this 'extended internal labour market', job information was usually passed to kin.

In China Wonder, the Finishing Unit supervisor took six years to weave his family network, connecting individuals to different work positions. Acting as a paternalistic patron, he needed not only to take care of his relatives and co-villagers' daily lives and accommodation, but also was responsible for their work behaviour on the shop floor. All the family members recruited need to be responsible, and this fact might have the effect of policing the performance of the worker; if the family members let the family down, they let the team down, and payment, which is strongly performance-based, would suffer. This resulted in mutual obligations, as well as mutual control and group discipline in the workplace. Thus, labour mobility was balanced by this self-regulated network, which served as a stabiliser, maintaining a constant labour force for the dormitory labour regime.

Freedom of movement

China Wonder stressed tight control and restrictive measures to regulate workers, who came from more than five provinces. The company kept the workers' identity card, as well as enforcing a system of deposits. In addition to the token Disney Code, China Wonder had its own code, the real one, which was far more detailed and disciplinary. After entering the company, every worker received a handbook which contained more than 50 provisions.

The working hours were very long; overtime work on Sundays and every night was expected. The workers in China Wonder worked from 8 a.m. to 10 p.m. If there were rush orders, the workers could be requested to work until midnight. Twelve working hours per day was normal for the workers; a rest day would be provided only if there was a break of production orders, or in the low season. This meant that the workers worked between 72 hours and 77 hours each week, far more than the working hours allowed by Chinese law (40 hours each week, and 36 hours' overtime work per month). It openly violated the Chinese Law and the Disney Code. At the beginning of 2002, the factory continued to operate on 1 January, the National Day, which was a statutory holiday. In addition, workers had to work on Sunday 24 February after the Chinese New Year holiday, which was in violation of the code providing one day off in seven.

According to Chinese law, overtime on normal workdays has to be paid at 150 per cent of normal wages, 200 per cent when on rest days, and 300 per cent during statutory holidays. Most of the workers would not know the Chinese labour law, since there were no educational or promotion programmes. Most workers, in particular those in the cutting, sewing, packing, and quality-control sections, were paid on a piece-rate basis. Other workers and apprentices were paid on an hourly basis, while management staff were on a monthly payroll. For those workers paid on a piece-rate basis, the overtime premium was paid according to the law as far as normal workdays were concerned. Wages for overtime during rest days, however, did not conform to the law. Work on Saturday was thus not considered overtime, which was classified only as Sunday work and work after 8 p.m. Overtime was paid at the 1.5 rate only.

The workers interviewed, for their part, did not have a clear understanding of when the overtime premium was paid, and were under the impression that overtime was paid only in the evenings, and not on Saturdays or Sundays, since both the company and the workers would take evening work as overtime work. Overtime work was not voluntary, as stipulated by Chinese law and the Disney Code. In contradiction of the law, the worker's handbook stated: 'When the workers cannot do overtime, they have to apply to the supervisors for a written exemption from overtime.' While the workers welcomed the possibility to work overtime, they considered that they could not refuse it, especially during the high season.

Wages in China Wonder were relatively high. However, workers received more only because of the excessive hours that they had to work. The paternalistic dormitory labour regime provided absolute lengthening of working hours, and double extraction of labour power through absolute control of labour time and living space.

Conclusion

Because of the obvious violations of the company codes and Chinese law in most of the transnational companies, the Chinese Working Women Network joined with the Clean Clothes Campaign in 2002 on a pilot project to set up a monitoring system in China. The precarious employment system in China has come about through a mixture of global, national, and local factors. These local particulars are often overlooked in the global trade analysis. The migration cycle, women's struggle against the patriarchal culture, and the huge rural–urban divide have contributed to women workers' acceptance of low-waged work in the city. The great labour surplus in China exacerbates this low-waged but efficient production system, suiting the 'race to the bottom' production strategies of capital. Local government has removed workers' basic labour and civil rights, and transferred the cost of labour reproduction to rural communities. The absence of residential rights has created a highly exploitative situation in which workers cannot easily organise themselves.

The dormitory labour regime houses more than one hundred million migrant workers in China. These workers are mostly young, single, and female, toiling twelve hours a day in garment, electronics and toy factories. Applying long and flexible labour hours, while incurring low production cost, and maintaining strict control over working lives, this dormitory labour regime is a new creation in China. Women workers' organisations are needed to safeguard workers' rights in a context where neither state nor capital is a genuine regulator of labour standards.

Pun Ngai is the President of the Chinese Working Women Network. She is also an anthropologist teaching at Division of Social Science, Hong Kong University of Science and Technology. sonpun@ust.hk

Notes

1 The women workers are recruited from the rural communities, where education, training, housing and the general welfare are provided. The reproduction of the next generation of labour is again shouldered by the rural villages which provide surplus labour.

2 No one can change his/her identity except under state planning. In some cases university graduates were allowed to change their *hukou* to work in big cities, because they were considered professionals.

References

Croll, Elisabeth (1985) *Women and Development in China: Production and Reproduction*, Geneva: International Labour Office.

Johnson, Kay Ann (1983) *Women, the Family and Peasant Revolution in China*, Chicago: the University of Chicago Press.

Smith, Chris and Ngai Pun, 'Putting the Transnational Labour Process in its Place: The Dormitory Labour Regime in Post-Socialist China', paper presented at International Labour Process Conference, Bristol, April 2003.

Solinger, Dorothy (1991) *China's Transients and the State: a Form of Civil Society?*, Hong Kong: Hong Kong Institute of Asia-Pacific Studies, the Chinese University of Hong Kong, p.8.

Solinger, Dorothy (1999) *Contesting Citizenship in Urban China*, Berkeley: University of California Press.

Being a female entrepreneur in Botswana:
cultures, values, strategies for success

Peggy Ntseane

This article elucidates a study of businesswomen as they move from owning and managing informal businesses into the formal economy. The study indicates that business success for rural women in Botswana is specific to the socio-cultural context. By examining prevalent concepts of patriarchy and community in our study, we start to see that cultural values frame successful business strategies. For Botswana women engaged in small business, non-competitive networks, collective management strategies, and informal cross-border trade are the pillars of sustainable business success.

In response to increasing poverty among women and children, feminist economic development theorists have begun to look at the social agency of women in their respective constraining environments. Post-modern economic feminists (Marchand and Parpart, 1995) have called for an approach to development that will acknowledge previously silenced voices, and welcome multiple solutions in development (Ward, 1998; Wolf, 1995; Kabeer, 1994).

In Southern Africa, the informal economy is a means of survival for many female-headed households, especially those in the urban areas. Activities in this sector include agriculture, small manufacturing, transport services, construction and trade, especially retail (International Labour Organisation 1992) and generate employment for urban people who would otherwise be unemployed (Maldonado, 1995).

An increasing number of Botswana women migrate from rural to urban areas for economic reasons. Although about 75 per cent of these women end up engaging in the informal sector, especially street vending, most of these small businesses never expand (Daniels, 1992). They either fail completely or remain in the initial stage of development.[1]

The limited empirical research on gender and development in the context of the Botswana economy has tended to focus on modern business-skills training, or the problems of female entrepreneurs. The latter include lack of capital, poor access to markets, lack of labour, and competition from men who have been pushed out of the formal sector by economic recession. Evidence from programme evaluations (International Labour Organisation, 1997) shows that business training alone does not guarantee successful entrepreneurship. This paper argues, first, that factors associated with social contexts are very influential in determining women's success or failure as entrepreneurs. Second, to support women who are trying to break into non-female traditional areas like formal businesses, development practitioners need to understand gender differences in the context of business strategy.

The study

The research study on which this paper is based came about because of a wish to understand how some women learn to move from unemployment in the rural areas of Botswana to owning successful small businesses in an urban setting. The research questions guiding this study focused on two areas of inquiry. First, what contextual and personal factors facilitate or impede the success of women's small businesses? And second, what is the common process that a woman in this culture typically goes through to build a successful business?

Methodology

Thirteen successful small-businesswomen from the cities of Francistown and Gaborone in Botswana were selected and interviewed in 1999.[2] Indicators of business success for this study included increases in annual revenues and investment expenditures, increase in the number of employees from one to ten or more, and status movement from an informal (unregistered) to formal (registered) business.

Participants ranged in age from 28 to 60 years, while their educational level ranged from three to twelve years of schooling. All had dependent children, but only four were married. All had been in business for at least eight years and employed ten or more workers at the time of the interview. These businesses included retail of agricultural produce (namely, vegetables and fruits), small manufacturing (especially sewing and upholstery businesses), small grocery stores, food take-away, hair salons, and boutiques.

The social context of women in Botswana

Botswana has taken steps towards bridging the gap between men and women in the social, economic, and political fields. This is evidenced by the adoption of the National Policy on Women and Development in 1996 and its accession to the Convention on the Elimination of all Forms of Discrimination Against Women (CEDAW) in 1998. However, gender inequality, especially as it relates to the business community, has persisted. Under Botswana law, most women in urban areas who are married under the 'in-community property option'[3] have the legal status of minors. Women cannot enter any legal binding contracts without the husband's consent or assistance, or register property in their own names (Molokomme, 1994; Grosh and Somolekae, 1996). This is likely to have negative impacts for the success of married women's small businesses. Furthermore, although 47 per cent of all families in Botswana are headed by single or unmarried women, women are under-represented in key decision-making positions and have limited control of resources. Cattle is a significant source of income, yet women owned only 14 per cent of all cattle in 1991 (Central Statistics Office, 1991). Women comprise 40 per cent of all workers in the cash economy. Of these, Chilisa (2001:10) observed that 'this large proportion of women is concentrated in the lower paid category and insecure jobs'.

As in most African societies, patriarchy reigns in Botswana, and women who engage in businesses are entrepreneurs and domestic servants for their families and society. Their labour is divided between domestic chores and business management. This has had a negative impact on their business performance, partly because women in the informal sector have not benefited from available training opportunities. Poverty, lack of power in the family and politics, and general under-representation in key decision-making positions have subjected women to marginalisation and violence. This article focuses on the strategies used by successful rural businesswomen to overcome these constraints.

The process of building a successful business

The study identified a common process which could explain the nature of women's success in small business in Botswana. The process commonly begins with non-normative behaviour. All of the participants traced the emergence and development of their business idea to a non-normative experience, such as teenage pregnancy, dropping out from school, or dysfunctional marriage. This triggered the need for money, since their behaviour had resulted in the loss of social support. In the case of divorced participants, for instance, women mentioned that they were left in a financially desperate situation. Faced with the need for money, participants realised that they had skills acquired from family, observation, or common sense, that they could use to start a business. All participants made a modest start to their businesses in the villages, selling very small commodities such as fat cakes, vegetables, and second-hand clothing. This start gave them the confidence to organise and manage business sales. They then made a move to the city to reach better markets. Participants' businesses expanded in the urban areas. In some cases, further growth allowed their businesses to market products back in the village, providing employment opportunities there.

The expansion often exposed them to the social injustices in their society. Crises and challenges confronting them, such as gender discrimination, lack of recognition for unregistered businesses, and discrimination in funding, had to be resolved in order for them to be successful in the city. Others experienced kidnappings and robbery ambushes in neighbouring countries while on business trips.

The use of networks was a feature of achieving success. For example, if a member's business experienced problems, others would assess the situation and help.

Findings of the study

Two issues were identified in the transition process experienced by small business-women in Gaborone and Francistown. Patriarchy and community orientation were cited as the contextual factors to be overcome, while social responsibilities were the personal factors. Secondly, business success had to be sustained through networking with family members, other businesswomen, and the larger community.

Contextual factors

Participants in this study agreed that, while women are not powerless, the balance of power is overwhelmingly in the men's favour. Betty's father described her hard work in this way: '*In Betty, God almost gave me a boy.*' Statements like this show that the society appreciates the qualities of hard work, intelligence, courage, and economic responsibility shown by businesswomen – but men still do not value women.

All the women had to get permission from their husbands, fathers, uncles, or even brothers to travel long distances to buy or sell their business products. Also, because of women's agricultural responsibility for domestic/family consumption, they perceive business outputs and profits as assets for sustaining the family. Most businesses fail or remain stuck at the initial stage mainly because businesswomen fail to separate business resources from family assets. One interviewee said, '*My business is a small grocery store. If I have no money to buy food, we get from the shop. If my relative's children have no food, I have to give them from the shop.*'

The social responsibility of women as caretakers, coupled with legislation that perceives them as minors or big girls, restricted the movements of all participants at the initial stages of their businesses. As Nana put it, '*What! Start a business in Gaborone? No! Being in business – even for single women – is something that you negotiate with the family, especially fathers and uncles.*'

Despite the drawbacks, community orientation was also described as an advantage. It involved sharing goods and services and decision-making processes based on group consensus, as explained by the Setswana proverb 'Motho ke motho ka batho ba bangwe' ('The individual is defined in a group context'). It is expected that people help others in the family or community. Women were helped by family and friends from their villages to settle in the city, and female family members assisted with child-care so that they could devote more time to the business.

Sharing among women has laid the foundation for mutually supportive strategies. Successful businesswomen whom we interviewed rejected the idea of competition, seeing it as a negative principle. Disadvantaged by gender inequalities, they claim they cannot operate individually, unlike their male counterparts. Almost all women mentioned that their success in business rests on sharing business ideas and profits, teaching and learning from others. Mma-Mak said, 'Success is not about making more and more money, but it is about what you can give to your family, community, and the business to sustain them.' Because of a cultural emphasis on communal survival, businesswomen see their businesses as a means of self-advancement as well as a contribution to society. On a practical level, women also rely on each other because of their lack of numeracy and their need for security.

All respondents identified social responsibility and resilience as the two personal factors crucial for success. They felt that being a responsible member of a community meant contributing to the welfare of their respective communities. 'Social responsibility' included being a mentor to other young women.

Resilience was required to be assertive with men. Examples cited included moving out of a marriage or telling male officers at government finance institutions that women's businesses were creating employment opportunities and should therefore benefit from government revenues. All described themselves as very persistent people with a strong will to take risks: from their experience, success and suffering go hand in hand. As businesswomen they suffered rejection by the larger society, for their economic independence did not sit well with men. Mma-Tebbie captured this when she said, 'The man that I had an intimate relationship with for 15 years said I was too independent to get married, because no man can control me.'

While social responsibility motivated the women to earn a living and create employment for other women, persistent resilience was needed to deal with gender inequality.

How businesswomen minimise barriers

As can be seen, two main factors were likely to impede success for women in business. These were patriarchal control and cultural pressure to behave in ways that counter good business sense. Women responded to these impediments by non-competitive networking and forming pressure groups.

Non-competitive networking was described as relying on one another for both business and family-related issues. At the family level, businesswomen in this study said they relied on their networks for moral support, free labour, information, and finance. Support was reciprocal, in that the business helped the family members directly or indirectly and was a first source of employment for family members. As Shadi said, 'I train my family members here in the business before I look for well-paying jobs for them. This is important, because as a family member if they mess up you cannot escape the humiliation.'

Reciprocal business relationships included giving one another material support. During slow periods of the year, women reported buying merchandise from one another and providing free labour. They also share ideas about commercial success, problem solving, and future planning. Adherence to community expectations of women could also become a strategy of sorts. Some participants exchanged business items in kind, in order to be perceived as behaving in a gender-appropriate way.

Some women reported that prior to formal registration of their businesses they had mobilised themselves into pressure groups to question unfair laws, harassment, requirements of commercial banks, and allocation of government tenders. They were also planning to organise to claim more access to credit facilities and markets.

Informal cross-border trade

Some women reported that regional networking took place in Southern Africa or even globally. One respondent explained that she did not have to carry cash when shopping for business in South Africa or Zimbabwe because, through business networks in these countries, she was able to open bank accounts. She said, '*These regional networks are crucial for the security of women business in this region.*'

Although men in the formal business sector also have local and regional business networks, for women, collective strategising and mutual support is a necessity. With minimal education, lack of resources, and a lower degree of independence, along with the need for security, businesswomen need each other for almost everything. Many women in similar businesses share venues but not customers. In the words of one respondent, '*We have to be near each other so that when the younger woman takes her child to the clinic I can remain selling for her. It would be mean for me to sit here and take her regular customers, just because her child is sick. As an older woman, I cannot travel long distances, but these young people buy vegetables cheaply for me in South Africa or Zimbabwe when they travel, and sometimes with their own money. So you never know when the other person will return the favour.*'

According to Sachikonye (1998), cross-border informal trading is a growing activity, driven by the effects of economic liberalisation and by high unemployment in the region. Participants in this study reported that businesswomen in cross-border trade deal directly with consumers. Furthermore, their markets are serviced by female networks in host countries in the region, to minimise the risks associated with female cross-border trade such as rape, theft, and other forms of harassment experienced at customs posts. Businesswomen attributed the financial success of their cross-border ventures to female networks which enabled them to trade goods without using foreign currencies.

Although findings of this study showed limited cross-border trade by successful businesswomen, studies of the informal sector in the region (Muzvidziwa, 1997; Gumbo and Mupedziswa, 1996) have found that it has been very effective in lifting some women out of poverty, because there is limited competition from poor men, who dominate the cross-border wage market instead. Unfortunately, women's cross-border trade is not reflected in national and regional trade statistics, probably because of its informal nature.

Conclusion: is success in business a value-free activity?

The pillar of women's small business success is seen to be informal, non-competitive networking. Business concepts are new in the Botswana culture, and there is confusion about how to interpret competition. However, the findings of this study suggest a difference between social capital in the capitalist business networks and Botswana women's business networks in the informal sector. For them, business networking is about the support that women in similar businesses can give to each other. They do not market products by lowering prices or improving the quality in order to compete on price. Unhealthy competition was described as competition that pushed other women out of business by not sharing ideas. '*I am able to feed the whole extended family and have created employment for 18 other women. I have to share the success experience with future mothers of my society.*' These findings on non-competitive networking support African feminist literature which refers to women's need to build on their traditional modes of organising in order to overcome the legacy of patriarchy in Africa (Mbilinyi, 1996; Oduol and Kabira, 1995).

Family and cultural values can play a contradictory role in women's business success, acting as a resource as well as an obstacle. However, successful Botswana women have been able to use cultural values to negotiate or resist patriarchal hegemony within the family. Participants in this study did not necessarily want their businesses to grow to medium size, because of the perceived gender discrimination in the formal sector. Instead, they said they wanted to share experiences with businesswomen in the informal sector so that the process of development could be made shorter and less frustrating for other women.

These findings have implications for development practice in the area of support for local trade ventures. Through collaborative and reciprocal competitive networks, small businesswomen in Botswana have a chance of success.

Dr Peggy Gabo Ntseane is a Senior Lecturer in the Department of Adult Education of the University of Botswana. She is trained as both an Adult Educator and a Sociologist. She is currently working on a research project on 'HIV/AIDS, Patriarchy and Poverty: A study of cultural and economic constraints on women and HIV/AIDS prevention'.
ntseanep@mopipi.ub.bw

Notes

1 Mead (1994) found that in Botswana, Kenya, Malawi, Swaziland, and Zimbabwe most micro-enterprises that started with one to four people never expanded. Actually fewer than one per cent of small businesses grow to employ more than ten workers.

2 Data collected from 13 articulate businesswomen in 1999 were analysed inductively, using the constant comparative method (Merriam, 1998; Dey, 1993). A combination of criteria sampling and snowball sampling was used to compose a sample. The semi-structured interviews lasted from one to two hours and were the major source of data for this study. Observation of the business operations recorded in the field notes was another source of data. Follow-up contact through member checks also generated supplementary data.

3 In-community property option means that a husband and wife each have an equal or 50 per cent entitlement of the property accumulated during marriage at the time of divorce. This is in contrast with out-of-community property option, which refers to separate ownership of property during marriage and divorce.

References

Central Statistics Office (1991) Population Census Report, Gaborone: Botswana Government Printer.

Chilisa, B. (2001) 'Research Within Post Colonialism: Towards a Framework for Inclusive Research Practices', unpublished research paper, Department of Educational Foundations of the University of Botswana.

Daniels, L. (1992) *Micro and Small-scale Enterprises in Botswana: Results of a Nation-wide Survey*, US Agency for International Development (USAID),

Gaborone: Micro Investments and Institutions (GEMINI) Project.

Dey, I. (1993) *Qualitative Data Analysis: A user-friendly guide for social scientists*, London: Routledge.

Grosh B. and G. Somolekae (1996) 'Mighty oaks from little acons: Can micro-enterprise serve as the seedbed of industrialization?' *World Development* 24(12): 1879-90.

Gumbo, P. and R. Mupedziswa (1996) 'Structural Adjustment and Women Informal Sector Traders in Harare', unpublished paper.

International Labour Organization (1992) *World Labor Report*, Geneva: ILO.

International Labor Organization (1997) '2nd Start Your Business Impact Evaluation Report: Uganda, Zambia and Zimbabwe', unpublished report.

Kabeer, N. (1994) *Reversed Realities: Gender hierarchies in development thought*, London: Verso Press.

Maldonado, C. (1995) 'The informal sector: legalization or laissez-faire?', *International Labor Review* 34(6): 705-25.

Marchant, M. H. and J. L. Parpart (1995) *Feminism Postmodernism Development*, London: Routledge.

Mbilinyi, M. (1996) 'Towards a trans-formative methodology of political economy in adult education: A critical Third World feminist perspective', in P. Wangoola and F. Youngman (eds.) *Towards a Transformative Political Economy of Adult Education: Theoretical and practical challenges*, Dekalb, IL: LEPS Press.

Mead, D. (1994) 'The contributions of small enterprises to employment growth in Southern and Eastern Africa', *World Development* 22(12): 1881-94.

Merriam, S. B. (1998) *Qualitative Research Case-study Research: Application in education*, San Francisco: Jossey-Bass.

Molokomme, A. (1994) 'Marriage, what every woman wants or civil death? The legal status of married women in Botswana' in A. Armstrong and W. Ncube (eds.) *Women and the Law in Southern Africa*, Harare: Zimbabwe Publishing House.

Muzvidziwa, V. (1997) 'Urban Women's Strategies to Deal with Impoverishment in Masvingo, Zimbabwe' (PhD thesis, Waikato University, New Zealand).

Oduol, W. and W. M. Kabira (1995) 'The mother of warriors and her daughter: the woman's movement in Kenya', in A. Basu (ed.), *The Challenge of Local Feminism: Women's movements in global perspective*, Boulder, CO: Westview Press.

Sachikonye, L. (1998) 'Labor Migration in Southern Africa', Harare: SAPES Trust.

Ward, K. B. (1998) 'Gender, industrial-ization, transnational corporations and development: An overview of trends and patterns', in C. E. Boss and E. Acosta-Belen (eds.) *Women in the Latin American Development Press*, New Town: Temple University Press.

Wolf, D.L. (1995) *Feminist Dilemmas in Fieldwork*, Boulder, CO: Western New Press.

Look FIRST from a gender perspective: NAFTA and the FTAA

Marceline White[1]

Advocates for gender and economic justice have been calling for gender and social-impact assessments of trade policies for the past seven years. In 2002, Women's Edge Coalition completed a Trade Impact Review (TIR), an economic and legal framework to analyse the ways in which women and men may be differentially affected by global trade and investment agreements. In 2003, the TIR was used to evaluate how the North American Free Trade Agreement (NAFTA) helped or harmed poor women in Mexico. This paper briefly summarises the TIR, the results of the case study, and the Women's Edge Coalition's Look FIRST (Full Impact Review and Screening of Trade) campaign to require the US government to conduct such assessments before completing trade agreements.

The USA has been a leading proponent of free trade, having negotiated more than 300 separate trade agreements and passed five major pieces of trade legislation since 1992.[1] As delegates from developing countries observed during the WTO meeting in Cancun, the reality of free trade has not always matched the rhetoric, particularly for the poor. Many developing country officials noted that before negotiating further trade liberalisation, it is important to assess where trade has helped the poor, and where it has hindered them.

The effect of trade on women, who make up the vast majority of the world's poorest citizens, must be carefully examined. If trade is to benefit the poor, there should be positive benefits for poor women, for whom a small increase in income could have an enormous impact.

Global trade and investment agreements

Trade agreements now extend to agricultural products, services such as the provision of health care, education, and water, and 'trade-related' areas such as intellectual property rights, government purchasing, and foreign investment. At the same time, more detailed rules have been and are being developed to reduce perceived structural and institutional impediments to trade, including domestic laws and regulations. Over the past two decades, there has also been a parallel trend in many countries to privatise industries and services formerly owned or provided by governments. One result is that many goods and services that have traditionally been provided by the public sector are now increasingly subject to competition from foreign companies. Moreover, national and local laws that have been enacted to promote economic development, human and labour rights, environmental protection, and the empowerment of women and other disadvantaged groups may now be challenged as barriers to trade.

Recently negotiated trade agreements also include stronger dispute-settlement provisions, which increase the likelihood that trade disputes between state parties will be decided by expert panels, rather than being resolved through informal means, and that the panels' recommendations will be enforced, if necessary, through the withdrawal of trade concessions by the complaining party. Multilateral, regional, and bilateral trade rules now have significantly sharper 'teeth' than other international commitments, a fact which gives state parties a strong incentive to adjust their laws and policies to conform to trade-panel decisions, even at the expense of other international commitments or other compelling domestic policies. Where state parties do not comply with trade-panel rulings, they risk substantial economic loss from the withdrawal of trade concessions (Gammage, Jorgensen, McGill, and White, 2002).

As the purview of trade agreements has expanded, so too have the concerns of civil society organisations. Trade agreements now affect areas of concern that once seemed far removed, such as environmental protection, labour rights and working conditions, sustainable development, and gender equality.

The need for social-impact assessments

Trade agreements are negotiated by government trade representatives with little input from civil society groups. The trade negotiators may have economic or legal expertise, but they often lack understanding of the direct and indirect impacts of their negotiations on the lives of the poor.

Policy makers need access to information about the potential benefits and drawbacks of trade pacts before ratifying them. Once an agreement is completed, developing countries often cannot afford to change a commitment, even if circumstances within the country, such as a financial crisis, health epidemic, or other critical issue, warrant a change. Yet few governments have attempted to consider the effects of trade or investment commitments on their citizens, or on their own ability to be flexible enough to make policy decisions in the public interest.

The United States does assess how an agreement may affect workers and the environment, but these analyses consider only the potential economic effects; they do not account for the effect of legal and regulatory changes which may be required to conform to a trade agreement.

Gender and trade

Women are disproportionately poorer than men, as a result of social and cultural discrimination which limits their access to education, technological training, credit, and land. In addition, women are not hired for many jobs for which they qualify; they are considered 'secondary' wage earners (unlike men, who are considered to require higher wages as 'primary' wage earners). Women often obtain less pay than men for the same or similar types of jobs, and are usually the last workers hired and the first fired. Women of child-bearing age may be discouraged from seeking certain types of job, or jobs in certain sectors that are considered inappropriate for pregnant women. In parts of rural Asia, North Africa, and the Middle East, women's mobility is limited after puberty and before the menopause. It is not considered appropriate for women to travel alone or without the accompaniment of a male relative. Furthermore, many women are in the labour market for fewer years than men, entering and leaving employment more frequently than men in order to care for children and older family members.

In addition, women still do the bulk of 'reproductive' work (work concerned with the care and upbringing of children) and this invisible work means that they have less time to gain new job skills, or seek new jobs. This undervaluing of women's labour also translates into an inability to command equal wages for equal work. Moreover, many women work in the informal economy, in part because it enables them to combine income-generating opportunities with their household responsibilities. Because of women's primary role as care-givers, their consumption patterns may differ from those of men. Household resources, including food, may be prioritised for wage earners, frequently men or boys. Furthermore, changes in the price of food, education expenses, or health care provision may affect women more than men. When prices rise or service provision declines, women may be required to compensate by expanding their role as care-givers.

Finally, race, class, ethnicity, and geography affect the ways in which women participate in the local, national, or global economy. Different job opportunities are available for women in urban and rural areas. Poverty-stricken urban women may find work as domestics or in export-processing zones, while rural women often work as agricultural workers or in the informal sector. Their location determines the number and kinds of employment options available to them. Indigenous women often face additional socio-cultural barriers to participation in the global economy. In Chiapas, Mexico, for example, 58 per cent of indigenous women aged 40–44 spoke only their indigenous language, compared with 22 per cent of indigenous men. The inability to communicate in Spanish limits these women's ability to find employment (Cunningham and Cos-Montiel, 2003).

In summary, trade agreements may directly change the types of work available for women, the conditions of work, and the wages for work. Moreover, trade agreements may indirectly affect women's lives by contributing to changes in infrastructure, government provisioning of services such as health care and education, and a reduction in trade tariffs which may alter a government's budget and spending.

Trade agreements may both create new gendered effects – such as creating new jobs, for example in export-processing zones, where women are the preferred employees – and perpetuate or exacerbate existing gender-based discrimination. For this reason, women's advocates have been calling for gender and social assessments of trade agreements for the past six years. Governments have been loathe to carry out such assessments, arguing either that the gendered impacts of trade are a social issue and therefore unrelated to trade, or acknowledging that women are differentially affected by trade and investment agreements, but stating that they do not know how to conduct such an assessment.

The Trade Impact Review

Women's Edge Coalition, a US-based coalition working on gender, development, and global trade policies, developed a Trade Impact Review (TIR) to examine how trade agreements can affect gender and development issues – including economic, social, cultural, and legal and regulatory frameworks, agreements, and policies.

The goal of the TIR was to prove that a framework could be developed which used readily available data and indicators, relied on studies that had been conducted, and (even if only partly completed) would provide policy makers with more information about how trade may have different consequences for poor men and women. The hypothesis is that policy makers, armed with this information, can change trade commitments which have demonstrably harmed the poor before further agreements are entered into.

The TIR framework was developed by two economists, a trade lawyer, and a policy advocate, and reviewed by a panel of development experts, economists, trade lawyers, and NGO leaders working on trade. It does not assume that trade will harm or benefit poor women. The TIR framework assesses the direct and indirect economic effects of a change in trade or investment policy, as well as the legal and regulatory changes or conflicts that a new trade policy may pose.

The TIR differs from other gender assessments in that it includes both economic and legal/regulatory analysis. The economic framework clearly illustrates that a policy change can set into motion a series of other economic changes that directly affect the livelihoods and well-being of women and men in the global South and the United States.

The legal and regulatory section of the framework employs both a content analysis and a conflict analysis, to ascertain possible gender-differentiated effects of trade and investment agreements. Looking at the content of a trade or investment commitment itself, policy makers should consider whether it contains any overtly gender-biased provisions. Another way to analyse the content of a commitment is to consider whether gender-neutral provisions might affect women differently. Finally, the analyst should consider whether the implementation or enforcement mechanisms of the agreement could disadvantage women (Gammage et al., 2002).

A conflict analysis would consider the possible interactions between proposed trade or investment commitments and the laws relevant to women in a particular country, including the array of formal and informal laws and norms that determine women's status and rights. For example, could the implementation of a trade or investment agreement undermine a trading partner's international commitments, such as those listed under the Convention on the Elimination of All Forms of Discrimination Against Women (CEDAW), or constitutional or statutory guarantees of gender equality?

The TIR includes a matrix which is organised sectorally so that a trade policy maker in charge of agriculture negotiations could review key studies, indicators, questions, and legal issues in order to gauge potential impacts of trade agreements on women prior to the completion of a trade agreement.

The 'Look FIRST' campaign

The TIR is the centrepiece of the Women's Edge Coalition's 'Look FIRST' (Full Impact Review and Screening of Trade) campaign. The goal of the campaign is to achieve the enactment of legislation requiring the US government to conduct a TIR before completing bilateral, regional, and multi-lateral trade agreements.

The proposed legislation requires the National Academy of Sciences (NAS), an independent research institution which often conducts studies for the US Congress, to conduct the reviews. The NAS is considered a non-partisan body. Congress cannot influence the selection of personnel assembled to conduct the TIR. The NAS works collaboratively with similar organisations in other countries.

In addition to providing new analysis about how a trade commitment may affect the poor, the legislation also states that stakeholders such as gender and trade experts, development experts, academics, indigenous group leaders, NGO leaders from other countries, and state and local officials should be among the group selected to conduct the TIR.

Research findings

After developing the TIR, the next step of the Look FIRST campaign was to conduct a pilot case study to demonstrate the TIR's utility. Then the TIR and case-study results would be discussed with the media, policy makers, legislators, and officials in the US administration.

After ten years' experience of free trade under the North American Free Trade Agreement (NAFTA), a trade agreement between the USA, Canada, and Mexico, Mexico was an ideal country to analyse in terms of how new trade rules affect the poor, and to forecast what deeper trade liberalisation under the FTAA would mean for them. Working with a Mexican economist who helped to develop the TIR, and *Mujeres Para Dialogo*, a Mexican women's NGO, Women's Edge Coalition conducted a case study of the economic and legal effects of NAFTA, and the potential impacts of the FTAA in Mexico.

The agricultural sector was the focus of the report. In Mexico, the majority of the poor are rural, subsistence farmers. Today 25 million people live in Mexico, and approximately 20 per cent work in the agricultural sector, where wages are lower than in other sectors and poverty rates higher.[2] Yet women own less than 20 per cent of all farmed land. Furthermore, when women do own land, they tend to own much smaller parcels than men. In 2000, 56 per cent of women farmers owned less than 2 hectares of land, whereas 35 per cent of male farmers owned similarly small parcels. Most women tend to use these small plots to grow food for their families' consumption and sell the excess. With such small farms, women farmers do not own enough land to grow crops for export. Therefore 56 per cent of women farmers cannot take advantage of the Mexican government's plan under NAFTA to grow crops for export (White, Salas, and Gammage, December 2003).

Proponents of NAFTA argued that the agreement would increase industrialisation in Mexico and make the agricultural sector more productive and efficient. Inefficient producers would find other employment, perhaps in the export sector, producing or processing vegetables, fruits, nuts, and coffee destined for the USA. Yet for subsistence producers the actual outcomes were devastating. NAFTA rules required the Mexican government to reduce price supports for domestic farmers and consumers and to reduce import restrictions. Small farmers were forced to compete with cheaper, imported crops from the USA. Farmers in the USA were able to benefit (and continue to benefit) from economies of scale as well as government subsidies.

Although NAFTA provided for a 15-year period in which to eliminate quotas for imported corn, Mexico eliminated its corn quotas within 30 months, because the government thought that it would be less expensive to purchase corn from the USA and because it believed that small corn producers would find new employment generated by NAFTA. In reality, small farmers could not compete with the subsidised US imports and were unable to find comparable jobs in rural areas where they lived. Real corn prices fell more than 70 per cent (from 732 *pesos* in 1994 to 204 *pesos* in 2001) since NAFTA began. Families are living on an income that is one-third of what they earned in 1994.

The fall in corn prices did not benefit urban consumers either. The government eliminated subsidies for tortilla mills, and prices rose by 50 per cent in Mexico City and by even more in rural areas.[3]

More than 1.3 million subsistence farmers left the sector when they could no longer afford to farm. Wages fell dramatically. Monthly income for self-employed farmers fell from an average of 1,959 *pesos* in 1991 to 228 *pesos* in 2003 (White et al., 2003).

For households headed by women, it was even worse. Quantitative analysis of national gender-disaggregated data revealed that poverty increased by 50 per cent in the poorest, female-headed households between 1992 and 2000 (ibid.). This may be due to the fact that in rural areas, women heads-of-households have fewer marketable skills and many of them enjoy lower education or employment opportunities than men.

For the very poor, poverty increased in urban areas as well. Between 1990 and 2000, men's average wages fell by 256 *pesos*, while women's fell by 76 *pesos* over the same period. However, women with a primary education had already been earning far less than men with similar educational backgrounds. Men's lowest wage of 701 *pesos* was still 67 *pesos* more than women's highest wage during that period.

To compensate for falling incomes, more women entered the workforce. Quantitative analysis of household survey data showed that in 2000, among the poorest families, more people had to work to earn the same amount as the family had made in 1992. In fact, the numbers of homes with three or more income-earners almost doubled between 1992 and 2000 (ibid.). Women's workloads increased as they worked outside the home, while having to maintain their household responsibilities.

Some women gained jobs in the non-traditional agricultural export (NTAE) sector, processing fruits and vegetables for export. Estimates for 2000 estimate total employment in this sector at 1,847,680 jobs, representing an approximate increase of 329,555 jobs since 1994, or 20 per cent of pre-NAFTA employment in the sector. Between 1994 and 2000, women gained 83 per cent of the new jobs in this sector, but earned 25–30 per cent less than men in comparable jobs. These jobs tend to be labour-intensive, requiring women to be on their feet all day, performing repetitive movements (Cunningham and Cos-Montiel, 2003) but they may be an improvement on work in the informal sector. Other women gained jobs in the export-processing industry, sewing garments or assembling electronic components for export to the USA. However, these jobs are precarious, low-waged, and do not enable women to pull themselves out of poverty (Corporate Watch, 1999). Now, many of those *maquila* jobs are leaving Mexico and going to China, where the wages are lower.

In urban areas, between 1992 and 2000, consumption patterns changed among poor households. Women cut back on food and began to purchase more food at cheaper, roadside stalls. Families reduced the amount that they were spending on food, health care, and clothing. Despite these cutbacks, families struggled to maintain their standard of living. In 1980, one ton of corn would purchase 6.1 baskets of basic goods; but by 2000, one ton of corn would purchase only 2.4 baskets of basic goods. The fall in prices is, of course, linked to the Mexico government's agreement to cut subsidies for corn and beans and accelerate the elimination of quotas for imported corn.

Finally, the economic analysis forecasts what jobs will be lost or gained in Mexico if the Free Trade Area of the Americas (FTAA) is ratified. The FTAA is a hemisphere-wide trade agreement which would extend NAFTA rules to all countries in North America, Central America, and South America, as well as the Caribbean. Mexico would compete for the US market against other large economies, such as Brazil and Argentina. The quantitative analysis forecast what employment gains and losses Mexico might expect if current job trends continued. If current employment trends continue, the best-case scenario is that 350,000 more jobs will be lost in a five-year period. In a worst-case scenario, this number could rise to 750,000.

As mentioned earlier, the TIR examines both the economic effects of a trade agreement and the legal and regulatory effects. The Mexican case study examines the effects of NAFTA laws on women's rights, indigenous rights, and social and cultural rights, and it suggests areas where the FTAA may improve or conflict with Mexican laws and covenants. The TIR found that under NAFTA gender-specific labour laws on matters such as non-discrimination and equal-pay standards were given secondary status in the North American Agreement on Labour Cupertino (NAALC) (Concha, Espinosa, and Martinez, 2004). This means that Mexico cannot convene a panel or withdraw trade benefits if women workers' rights are violated. Given that there have been well-documented cases of sexual harassment and forced pregnancy-testing in the export-processing zones, this oversight is a serious concern (ibid.). Women working in export-processing zones have no avenue to redress their grievances if the corporation or individual that owns the factory is foreign.

The case study also found that neither NAFTA nor the FTAA recognised the constitutional guarantees of indigenous peoples. The Convention on Biological Diversity (which Mexico signed) states that 'Each Contracting Party, as far as possible and appropriate, shall introduce appropriate procedures requiring environmental impact assessments of its proposed projects that are likely to have significant adverse effects on biological diversity with a view to avoiding or minimising such effects and, where appropriate, allow for public participation in such procedures' (ibid.).[4]

Despite the important role that indigenous people play in protecting and caring for biodiversity zones and fragile flora and fauna, the Mexican government has not conducted environmental-impact assessments for the FTAA, nor consulted with indigenous groups in any meaningful way about the potential impact of the FTAA on their lives or on the environment in which they live.

Furthermore, the legal analysis showed that the Intellectual Property Rights section of the FTAA conflicts with the protection of traditional knowledge. The Mexican government has committed itself to the protection of traditional knowledge of indigenous groups (ibid.). Yet the proposed text on intellectual property in the FTAA grants exclusive rights to one owner of an idea, pattern, or other knowledge for up to 20 years (White and Spieldoch, 2003). The text does not recognise community and/or indigenous ownership of knowledge. Knowledge of certain plant uses, craft production, and traditional music or folklore is passed down from one generation to the next within a community (ibid.). There

is to date no appropriate legal mechanism in IPR to protect significant designs and symbols that belong to entire indigenous cultures.

Because indigenous knowledge is not protected, corporations could patent flora and fauna found in bio-diverse regions in Latin America which indigenous groups have used for centuries. The indigenous groups would not receive any profits from their knowledge.

Similarly, corporations could patent indigenous designs used on ceramics, woven items, or sewn items and not compensate indigenous groups. This is a critical issue for indigenous artisans. Women handicraft producers who make and sell their textiles, jewellery, and ceramics locally and globally comprise 70 per cent of craft workers in Latin America.[5] Crafts production celebrates indigenous culture and enables women to earn an income while they are caring for their children and maintaining their households. Mass-produced, cheaply made imitation baskets from China have already harmed the livelihoods of 20,000 Taharumara Indians in northern Mexico.[6] The vast majority of Taharuma Indian weavers are women, whose craft sales supplement their family's agricultural income.

Using the research

Using the TIR framework, Women's Edge Coalition, in collaboration with a Mexican economist and women's group, was able to show that NAFTA affected men and women differently. Realistic policy recommendations flow from the TIR, including exemptions for small, subsistence farmers under NAFTA and in the FTAA; increased training programmes for displaced farmers; increased investments in education and adult education; and market creation for niche products and fairly traded products. The case study also demonstrated that the TIR could be done quickly and inexpensively. With only

$150,000 and a time period of six months, Women's Edge Coalition was able to conduct the TIR in Mexico.

Women's Edge Coalition and *Mujeres Para Dialogo* held a briefing for Members of Congress about the results of the case study. Staff from more than 50 offices attended the meeting. The case study was also presented to staff at the US Department of State and US Agency for International Development. In addition, Women's Edge Coalition gathered 4,000 letters addressed to Bob Zoellick, the chief negotiator for trade in the USA, requesting that the TIR be systematically used to assess the gender and social-development impacts of all future trade agreements.

The organisation is in the process of introducing the Bill into Congress and building organisational and grassroots support for the 'Look FIRST Act of 2004'. In the meantime, the case study and TIR have already affected policy. In a concession to US women and development groups, the Office of the US Trade Representative (USTR) has agreed to disaggregate the labour analysis of the US–Chile agreement, as well as the Central America Free Trade Agreement (CAFTA). This was completed in July 2003. The CAFTA analysis, scheduled for completion in April 2004, should include some discussion of women's rights and working conditions in export-processing zones and flora culture.

Although the proposed legislation does not promote a particular perspective on trade, some ardent proponents of free trade believe that anything which slows down a trade agreement is bad, even if it does provide more facts and insight into the potential effects of the agreement.

If it is passed, we hope that the 'Look FIRST Act' and the TIR will create a process in which broader questions of the impact of trade are deliberated and resolved by a wide range of stakeholders, rather than just a few trade negotiators. Then, perhaps, trade agreements really will be crafted to serve as

a tool for development. A thorough analysis of how they may affect poor women could yield policy recommendations which would enable women to benefit from trade. The Look FIRST campaign could lead to outcomes such as niche marketing for products grown and processed by women; an increase in purchases of fair-trade products, particularly crafts and commodities produced by women's co-operatives; increased support for adult education and retraining programmes for women who have been displaced by trade; and a more sustained analysis of the quality of work available to poor women, as well as the number of jobs available to them.

Marceline White directs the Global Trade Program at Women's Edge Coalition. She has developed and written the gender analysis of the FTAA for a hemispheric coalition working on regional trade agreements. She also has expertise in the areas of women's work in the maquiladoras in El Salvador; refugee women and reproductive health; and women and political organising in Central America.
www.womensedge.org

Notes

1 Ambassador Charlene Barshefsky, US Trade Representative: 'Toward the Free Trade Area of the Americas: The Record and Future of Hemispheric Integration', Council of the Americas, Washington DC, 2 May 2000.

2 Secretaria del Trabajo y Prevision Social (2000), Estatistical Laborales, Cuarto Trimestre 2000, Coordination General de Politicas, Estudios y Estadisticas del Trabajo, Mexico.

3 'Tortilla Price Hike Hits Mexico's Poorest', *Washington Post*, 12 January 1999.

4 The Convention on Biological Diversity, Article 14. Impact Assessment and Minimising Adverse Impacts, on the worldwide web: www.biodiv.org/convention/articles.

5 'The Craft of Sustainable Development', Americas, Washington: Organisation of the American States, 1999.

6 Carlos Coria Rivas: 'Pirated handicrafts put Tarahumaras in danger', *The Miami Herald*, International Edition, 2 September 2003.

References

Concha, Leonor Aida, Rocio Corral Espinosa, and Miriam Martinez (2004) 'Trade Impact Review: Legal and Regulatory Analysis of NAFTA and the FTAA on Women's Rights', Washington DC: Women's Edge Coalition.

Corporate Watch, www.corpwatch.org, 30 June 1999.

Cunningham, Wendy and Francisco Cos-Montiel (2003) 'Crossroads of Gender and Culture: Impediments to Development in Chiapas, Guerrero, and Oaxac', The World Bank.

Gammage, Sarah, Helene Jorgensen, Eugenia McGill, with Marceline White (October 2002) 'Trade Impact Review', Washington DC: Women's Edge Coalition.

White, Marceline, Carlos Salas, and Sarah Gammage (November 2003) 'Trade Impact Review: Mexico Case Study, NAFTA and the FTAA: A Gender Analysis of Employment and Poverty Impacts in Agriculture', Washington DC: Women's Edge Coalition.

White, Marceline and Alexandra Spieldoch (January 2003) 'Analysis of the Free Trade Area of the Americas Text from a Gender Perspective', Washington DC: Hemispheric Social Alliance.

Are trade agreements with the EU beneficial to women in Africa, the Caribbean, and the Pacific?

Karin Ulmer

Economic Partnership Agreements (EPAs), currently being negotiated between the European Union and 77 African, Caribbean, and Pacific (ACP) countries, are due to enter into force in January 2008. These talks come under the umbrella of the 2000 Cotonou Partnership Agreement, which sets out a clear and specific commitment to gender equality. Despite this, gender issues are conspicuous by their absence from the 'hard' areas of the negotiations, such as trade and regional co-operation. In order to estimate the likely impact of future trade agreements on poor women and men, a more systematic approach to trade policy negotiations and to capacity building in ACP countries is required.

The Cotonou Partnership Agreement differs significantly from the Lomé Convention, which it succeeded. Although it still contains a commitment to reduction and elimination of poverty, there is a stronger emphasis on integrating the African, Caribbean, and Pacific (ACP) states into the global economy. The Economic Partnership Agreements (EPAs) are designed to speed up this process by reducing or ending preferential treatment of ACP exports to the European Union (EU), and between ACP countries themselves.

The second key aspect of the Cotonou Partnership Agreement is that civil society is to be informed and consulted about decisions on aid, and the economic, social, and institutional reforms that the EU intends to support. It is in this area that APRODEV[1] and other non-state actors can play a vital role in helping to shape policy.

APRODEV's Zimbabwe case study (Mugabe, Okore, and Ulmer 2002) identified the likely effects of EPAs and argued for

capacity building of women's organisations and civil society groups more generally, to ensure them a voice in trade policy making. Given the political events in Zimbabwe, advocacy positions since the research have not been further formulated. However, a number of aspects of the Zimbabwe case study are relevant to women in other ACP countries, as well as to policy makers and trade negotiators. The findings of the APRODEV study have also been used to provide input in the EU's Sustainability Impact Assessments and have provided background information for discussions on EPAs and women in West Africa.

What's new about Economic Partnership Agreements?

The current EPA negotiations are not simply about future conditions of access to the EU market, but about extending exclusive trade preferences to the EU.

Even though ACP countries have agreed to engage in these talks, they remain uncertain about how far EPAs will benefit their economic transformation, or affect their competitiveness once free trade arrangements are in place. There is some suspicion about how 'free' the trade arrangements will be, given the distorting effects of agricultural subsidies under the EU's Common Agricultural Policy (CAP). There is also a widespread fear that rejection of the EU's proposals may mean that they risk losing all or part of their aid allocations.

The EU wants EPA negotiations to go beyond tariffs and trade, to include a wide range of trade-related issues such as tourism, financial services, telecommunications, competition policy, intellectual property rights, labour standards, and consumer policy. The European Commission has explicitly said that it wants discussions to go beyond existing WTO commitments. But virtually all ACP governments lack the capacity to take up this negotiating challenge.

From a one-way to a two-way street

The European Commission strongly favours a radical transformation of ACP–EU trade relations, from a system of non-reciprocal to reciprocal trade preferences. This means that the EU will have preferential access to ACP markets, while goods from ACP countries have preferential access to EU markets. The Commission favours this shift because it wants to ensure that future ACP–EU trade relations are compatible with WTO standards. It claims that under the previous arrangements ACP countries have failed to deliver better industrial or trade outcomes, or to achieve development objectives.

It is not entirely accurate, however, to claim that the ACP countries' development objectives were not addressed under preferential arrangements with the EU. For example, between 1980 and 1997, prior to the current economic crisis, Zimbabwe was one of the most successful ACP countries in taking advantage of improved access to the EU market. From 1992 to 1996, Zimbabwean agricultural and horticultural exports rose by 35 per cent. In 1998 the sugar sector alone saw an estimated income transfer to Zimbabwe of more than 18 million euro, an amount greater than the annual aid allocation to Zimbabwe under the Lomé Convention (Netherlands Economic Institute Study 2000).

APRODEV has raised concerns over the ability of the new EPAs to contribute to the eradication of poverty. They could instead result in free trade which benefits the EU, but produces very few long-term advantages for the ACP countries. These countries start from a low base: an unhealthy and poorly trained workforce, inadequate transport infrastructure, and weak institutional and policy frameworks. They are vulnerable to agreements with the developed world which are not in the longer-term interest of their people, especially women, who are the backbone of agricultural production.

It is vital that existing sub-regional initiatives in Africa continue to be the basis for economic development. As it is not a 'level playing field', ACP states need to develop tough negotiating strategies, and to co-operate much more closely with one another. Under the Southern African Development Community (SADC) agreement, for example, Zimbabwean food producers have free access to the large South African market. It will be difficult for Zimbabwean food exporters to compete with EU products once the EU also has free access to the Southern African markets in 2010, as stipulated in the EU–South Africa Trade Agreement. This is a strong incentive for Zimbabwe's food-processing industry to become competitive with the EU over the next few years. However, it remains to be seen whether or not this can be achieved.

What's in it for women? The case of Zimbabwe

If official negotiators on both the EU and ACP sides focus only on macro-economic and political implications of trade, they could fail to address the implications for different social and economic groups. As has happened in the past, the burden of EPA reforms could fall heavily on women. In Zimbabwe, the 1990s Economic and Structural Adjustment Programme (ESAP) resulted in some negative trends for women. Women's employment in the formal sector declined by 9.5 per cent in the first year, and only 6 per cent of jobs created under employment schemes went to women, with only 11 per cent of loans going to small and medium-sized enterprises (SMEs) (ZWRCN, 1998). SMEs have proved to be an important area for the economic and social empowerment of women world-wide, but greater liberalisation under EPAs may reduce their capacity to compete with foreign goods and services.

Women are seriously disadvantaged by restricted access to productive resources and gaps in training and technology transfer. In Zimbabwe, most households are headed by women, and 74 per cent of these are poor, whereas 54 per cent of households headed by men are regarded as poor (Ministry of Public Service 1995). Eighty per cent of the rural population depends on agriculture, and women farmers are doubly disadvantaged. Women are allocated the worst and smallest pieces of land, and only 11.8 per cent of all land is controlled by women. Women access only 19.8 per cent of available oxen and 23.3 per cent of available credit to purchase seeds and fertilisers (ZWRCN 1994).

In general, past experiences of ACP–EU co-operation show that gender inequality has not been addressed. A 1997 review of 24 EU-funded development projects in ACP countries found that 21 in no way addressed gender inequalities (European Commission 1997). A 2002 Review of EU Country Strategy Papers and aid allocations concluded that gender mainstreaming was hardly taken up in country analysis or strategies in vital sectors such as transport, food security, and rural development (European Commission 2002).

The example of value-added food processing

In Zimbabwe, agriculture is not only essential to individual survival but also the backbone of the economy. It provides 45 per cent of the country's exports, 60 per cent of all raw materials used by its industry, and employment for 70 per cent of the population. Seventy-one per cent of the total female population gains employment from the farming of communal areas. Women comprise 70 per cent of smallholder grain farmers, and maize is an important source of household cash income for them, as well as being a basic crop for household food security (Statistical Bulletin 2001).

The 'value-added' food industry in Zimbabwe is an important part of the industrial sector and an important market for locally produced agricultural products. A wide range of food products is produced, including breakfast cereals, biscuits, milk- and sugar-based products, canned fruit and vegetables, and a wide variety of processed meat products. These industries absorb a significant proportion of the locally produced agricultural products from both communal and commercial farmers. Communal farmers (largely women) supply the local food-processing industry with maize, cotton, peanuts, sunflowers, and paprika, while commercial farmers supply sugar, soya beans, wheat, and pigs.

The EU's Common Agricultural Policy reform in the cereal sector has reduced EU cereal prices by 45 to 50 per cent since 1992. It has also led to an 18 per cent expansion of EU cereals production and cereal-based exports from 1991 to 2000 (European Commission 1992–2000). The CAP reform process will affect the market conditions facing ACP producers of competing products, and this in turn will affect their incomes at different stages of agricultural production, processing, and marketing. The impact is likely to be felt most heavily by women.

Any trade arrangements which allow the import of cheap subsidised maize or other cereal at prices which undermine local prices are likely to depress rural household incomes. Free trade in maize, cereals, and related products needs to be carefully structured to maximise income opportunities for women in rural areas. Cereals and cereal-based products would need to be subject to special trading arrangements, safeguard mechanisms and special protocols, as with the SADC Free Trade Area. Free trade with the EU is hugely distorted by subsidies to EU farmers. In the case of Zimbabwe, as with other ACP countries, there is a real danger that the deals on offer will damage regional food-processing industries, and women will bear a disproportionate cost.

Ethical trade makes sound commercial sense
The Zimbabwe case study also looked at the expansion of the cut flower sector under current preferential access to EU markets. In this sector, 83 per cent of the permanent workforce and 90 per cent of the seasonal workforce are female (Okore 2001). These women have been the principal beneficiaries of improvements to wages and working conditions resulting from preferential market access to the EU. Cut-flower producers and exporters got together to ensure compliance with quality standards and created a body to uphold the principles of the 'Agricultural Ethics Assurance Association of Zimbabwe', which covers about 31 per cent of the workers of this sector. This ethical trade initiative has supported improved labour conditions for women working on farms. With premium prices being paid in the EU for 'ethically produced' flowers, the growers

have found improved labour conditions beneficial to production efficiency and financial returns. This case demonstrates that fairer labour practices have the potential to bring social and economic gains at the household level, while making sound commercial sense. The research found that any loss of preferential access to the EU market in the cut-flowers sector will adversely affect women. Future trade arrangements should secure and maintain favourable conditions of access to the EU market.

Threat to new regional export opportunities
Under the current SADC protocol, Zimbabwe's sugar industry can exploit the protected and high-priced refined sugar market, with positive spin-offs in terms of female employment. Women are predominantly employed in the packing operations for refined sugar. Zimbabwe is potentially a competitive exporter to the Eastern and Southern African (ESA) market for value-added sugar products. Should free trade with the EU be introduced in the sugar sector, this could pose a real threat to the expansion of Zimbabwe's refined sugar exports to the Southern and Eastern African region.

Under current CAP reform, European producers in these sectors receive direct aid, which results in lower prices for their sugar and beef. European agro-business and exporters will be most likely to benefit from low prices and increased exports to ACP markets. In the face of this competition, Zimbabwe may not be able to take advantage of opportunities to export sugar and beef to regional markets, and women will lose opportunities for employment in value-added products in the beef sector.

The need for informed, gender-aware policy

The ACP–EU trade agreements need to incorporate an understanding of the constraints faced by women that make it difficult for them to benefit from trade arrangements. These include low levels of technical capacity and funds, as well as infrastructure and market standards which currently limit or inhibit women's capacity to engage with trade opportunities.

The implications of trade distortion resulting from EU agricultural subsidies also need to be recognised, and sensitivity to existing local and regional markets needs to be reflected in agreements. To take the Zimbabwean example, future trade agreements relating to maize could ensure that income opportunities for women in rural areas are maximised, not lost.

As a signatory to the Millennium Development Goals, the EU has committed itself to halving the number of people living in extreme poverty in developing countries by 2015. Future trade regimes will have to be measured against this objective. Improved access to the EU markets is of benefit to the huge female workforce in ACP countries, especially in agriculture. It is therefore essential that the progressive opening up of international markets takes into consideration the impacts on women. If future ACP–EU trade arrangements do not improve the position of women, then they do not materially improve the situation of the poorest people.

Karin Ulmer is the Policy and Gender officer at APRODEV, where she has worked since 2000. In that time she has worked on the gender/social impact of the EU–ACP trade negotiations (EPAs) and EU gender mainstreaming policies and practices. karin@aprodev.net

Notes

1 Association of World Council of Churches related development organisations in Europe, a network of 17 major development organisations in Europe.

References

European Commission (2002) 'Assessment of Country Strategy Papers with Reference to Gender', Brussels: EC.

European Commission, Directorate General for Agriculture (1992–2000) 'Agricultural Situation in the European Union', Successive Annual Reports 1992–2000, Brussels: EC.

European Commission (1997) 'Integrating Gender Issues in Development Cooperation: Progress Report 1997', Brussels: SEC (97) 2067.

Ministry of Public Service, Labour and Social Welfare (1995) Survey, Harare, Zimbabwe, Central Statistical Office.

Mugabe, N., M. Okore, and K. Ulmer (2002) 'EPAs – What's in it for Women? Women in Zimbabwe: Issues in future trade negotiations with the EU', Brussels: APRODEV.

Netherlands Economic Institute Study (2000) 'Evaluation of the Common Organisation of the Markets in the Sugar Sector', CEC, Annex A3, Rotterdam.

Okore, M. (2001) 'Survey: Aggregated Data based on Individual Farm Report Sheets from the Agricultural Ethics Assurance Association of Zimbabwe' (unpublished), Harare, Zimbabwe.

Statistical Bulletin (2001) Harare, Zimbabwe: Central Statistical Office.

ZWRCN (Zimbabwe Women's Resource Centre and Network) and the Southern African Research and Documentation Centre (1994) 'The Gender Dimension of Access and Land Use Rights in Zimbabwe', Harare, Zimbabwe.

ZWRCN (1998) 'Beyond Inequalities: Women in Zimbabwe', Harare, Zimbabwe.

TRIPS and biodiversity:

a gender perspective

Suman Sahai

Gene Campaign is a movement involving organisations across Asia, working towards food and livelihood security for rural and tribal communities. It is deeply concerned about the negative impacts of privatisation on genetic resources through patenting and intellectual property rights. Biological resources are the mainstay of the livelihoods and local economies of communities in developing countries. Ensuring access to these resources is essential to their being able to engage in self-reliant growth. Women who are closely involved with the maintenance of biological resources are also its most sophisticated users, in feeding and looking after their families. The privatisation of these resources would undermine the ability of women to care for their families and seriously jeopardise the health and security of rural and tribal populations.

Traditionally, women have played an important role in managing the genetic diversity in their ecosystems. Their role has included harvesting carefully and allowing regeneration, so that the resource base is sustained over generations. In many Asian societies, field operations like ploughing and marketing are done by men, and the selection and storage of seed, planting and weeding in fields, by women. Women generally use their knowledge of natural and biological resources to satisfy multiple household needs. They breed well-adapted varieties and develop sophisticated farming systems, using a range of crop varieties, to ensure food and nutrition for the family. Their access to and use of genetic resources is unhindered, and they succeed in making effective use of them for food, fodder, medicine, and other essential products (GTZ 2002).

The transformation of agriculture to meet the needs of a globalising market economy is contributing to the steady erosion of the biological resources and knowledge systems controlled by women. The trend towards monocultures and cash crops in a high-input, intensive agriculture system, to produce crops on contract for urban and export markets, is having a negative impact on women's role in domestic and local arenas (NGO Women's Forum 2002).

Women and the conservation of biodiversity

Communities often have well-defined gender roles that apply to the work involved in plant and seed selection and storage. Traditionally women in Asia often use a variety of indigenous plants, trees, and animals, and they have a direct stake in conservation. Women tend to take a lead role in preserving and conserving croplands, forests, and other natural resources for perpetual use, while men are more likely to be involved in converting these resources into cash. Women are also often the traditional caretakers of genetic and species diversity in agriculture. Their knowledge of growing conditions and the nutritional characteristics of various species is an essential basis for seed selection and plant breeding. In many societies, it is women who are mainly responsible for this, as well as for seed exchange and preservation of local biodiversity (Rani and Swaminathan 1998).

The 'Convention on Biological Diversity' (CBD), which affirms the sovereign rights of nations over their bio-resources, calls for conservation of biodiversity, sustainable use of its components, and fair and equitable sharing of benefits arising from their utilisation. In the Preamble of the CBD, the central role of women in conserving biodiversity is recognised in the following declaration: 'affirming the need for the full participation of women at all levels of policy-making and implementation for biological diversity conservation'. Agenda 21, adopted at the Earth Summit in Rio de Janeiro in 1992, also stresses the need to strengthen women's involvement in national ecosystem management and control of environmental degradation.

Other international plans of action have highlighted the critical role of gender in genetic resources conservation and sustainable utilisation. The Food and Agriculture Organisation (FAO) publication, *Gender – Key to Sustainability and Food Security*, states: 'Rural women in developing countries hold the key to many of the planet's agriculture systems for food production, seed selection, and protection of agro-bio diversity' (Krishna 1998: 36).

The participants at a meeting convened by the International Plant Genetic Resources Institute (IPGRI) and FAO in Rome in October 1996 concluded, 'An understanding of men and women farmers' differential roles and responsibilities in PGR conservation and management, as well as the intrinsic value of their knowledge, is crucial to sustainable, effective and equitable PGR conservation and utilisation' (Sreenivasan and Christie 2002: 5).

The commercialisation of bio-resources

In recent decades there has been a distinct shift in the perception of biological resources. What was a 'natural' resource, accessible to all, has now become an 'economic' resource, to be privatised. In this process, public property jointly held and nurtured by communities is increasingly converted to private property, owned by a few and withheld from local communities.

This shift can be seen in recent international and national developments. Two major international agreements, the Agreement on Trade-Related Aspects of Intellectual Property Rights (TRIPS) of the WTO, and the United Nations Convention on Biological Diversity (CBD), with mutually conflicting approaches, are now shaping the domestic regimes of member states with respect to biological resources and associated indigenous knowledge. The Agreement on TRIPS engenders privatisation of biological resources by allowing patents to be granted on biological materials and associated indigenous knowledge. Meanwhile, the CBD acknowledges that local communities have rights over bio-resources and indigenous knowledge (Sahai 2003).

Biological diversity has become sought-after raw material for the life sciences industry. While corporations in the developed world have mastered the techniques of recombinant DNA technology, the raw matter is located principally in the tropical and semi-tropical countries of the developing South. Not only the resources, but the associated knowledge of their properties is located within indigenous communities.

In order to gain access to biological resources, the life-science corporations, through their governments, have extended the scope of intellectual property rights to biological materials at the global level. This development took place in the Uruguay GATT Round, which began in 1986 and concluded in Marrakech in 1994. During this round, life forms and genetic resources were brought into the ambit of one system for intellectual property rights (Sahai 2000).

Intellectual property rights over biological materials

The essential element of the TRIPS Agreements related to agriculture and food security is the requirement for WTO members to make patents available for any technological inventions, whether products or processes. One reason for greater interest in patents is the rapid development of biotechnology in agriculture.

There are four options within Article 27.3(b). First, to allow patents on everything. This would include all materials and all forms of technology. Second, to exclude plants, animals, and biological processes, but not plant varieties. This means that whereas naturally found plants, animals, and the natural biological process by which they are created could be excluded from patents, crop varieties could not. The third option is to exclude plants, animals, and biological processes from patenting and to introduce a special *sui generis* for the protection of plant varieties. A *sui generis* system allows a country to create a system of its choice which would enable the minimum protection agreed to in the WTO. The final option is to exclude plants, animals, and biological processes from patenting but not plant varieties, and to provide a *sui generis* right. This last would mean that plant varieties could be patented or protected by an independently created *sui generis* system (Leskien and Flitner 1997).

Most developing countries have chosen the third option. A *sui generis* system of protection is one adapted to particular subject matter; it allows countries to make their own rules for protection of new plant varieties. One possible *sui generis* system likely to be recognised is the International Union for the Protection of New Varieties of Plants (UPOV) system. This was initially developed in Europe and has now been adopted by the industrialised countries. The UPOV system has undergone several changes after its formulation in 1961, but these have resulted in almost no concessions for farmers and plant breeders in the South (Balakrishna 2000).

Article 27.3(b) of TRIPS is perhaps the most controversial clause of the entire WTO agreement (Sahai 2001). It requires members to provide for the patenting of 'non-biological and microbiological processes', and WTO members are now in the process of defining their positions regarding the future of the provisions. There are indications that a few members, like the USA, would like the *sui generis* option to be eliminated altogether, while most developing countries are preparing national legislation to implement it. There are proposals to treat UPOV as the only *sui generis* option for plant varieties. The problem is that UPOV is not in the interests of developing countries, since it does not contain any rights for farmers. There is only the right granted to the breeder, which in today's context is increasingly 'the company'. Patents on seeds would severely restrict farmers' access to them, since they would have to buy fresh seed for every sowing. Women would be particularly disadvantaged under UPOV, since their current access to their own seeds ensures that they can contribute to food, health, and nutrition for the household.

There are potential conflicts between the TRIPS patenting regime and the Convention on Biological Diversity (CBD), as well as the International Treaty on Plant Genetic Resources (ITPGR) of the FAO. These conflicts are widely seen as more political than legal in nature, and the US government has made early implementation of TRIPS a top priority of its foreign policy (Mulvany 1999). These matters are likely to emerge as matters of dispute under the WTO's dispute settlement system in the coming years.

UPOV 1991 conditions will significantly diminish the farming community's capacity to be self-sufficient in seed and self-reliant as agricultural producers (Sahai 2002a). UPOV requires plant varieties to be 'distinct' from other varieties, produce genetically 'uniform' progeny, and remain genetically 'stable' over generations. After the 1991 UPOV amendment, a new quality – 'novelty'– has been added to the minimal characteristics required. The uniformity requirement has potential to contribute to genetic erosion. In addition, the cost of maintaining UPOV certification is beyond the means of most farmer/breeders. Although peasant farmers have also cultivated plant varieties expressing desirable traits over time, their varieties rarely meet the UPOV requirements.

These conditions for a 'Plant Breeders' Right certificate' under UPOV run contrary to the goal of enhancing genetic diversity. Furthermore, the kind of protection that it grants is an exclusive monopoly right. This contrasts sharply with the broader goals of collective remuneration and benefit sharing that are expressed in a number of other global agreements.

UPOV conflicts with self-reliant agriculture and livelihood security

Most developing countries are contemplating the *sui generis* route to comply with TRIPS, instead of patenting. A number of influential bodies, including the WTO itself, are pushing for a narrowing of the *sui generis* option to one legislative model provided by the UPOV. Independent legal and economic experts have reiterated that UPOV should not be accepted as an effective *sui generis* system for TRIPS, and that there is ample scope for manoeuvre, flexibility, and national discretion in interpreting the *sui generis* option (Gaia Foundation–GRAIN 1998 and Gene Campaign–CEAD 1998).

The UPOV system promotes commercially bred plant varieties for industrial agricultural systems. Plants are bred to grow successfully with their chemical inputs or with their patented genes, at the expense of more sustainable bio-diverse systems. Since 'Plant Breeders' Rights' (PBRs) are given only for a variety that is genetically uniform, they limit both what kinds of seed can be marketed and who can market them. UPOV automatically discourages genetically diverse and locally adapted seeds from the market and from the field.

The impact of UPOV-type regimes will be highly detrimental to developing countries. First, farmers who have contributed the varieties on which plant breeders base their new varieties would have no rights. Secondly, UPOV laws favour countries where agriculture is largely a commercial activity. For the majority of farmers in Asia, Africa, and Latin America, however, it is a livelihood.

Applying the TRIPS framework to bio-resources is against the interests of indigenous and farming women and men (Sahai 2002b). It fails to acknowledge or protect farmers' rights, explicitly recognised in the CBD and ITPGR. In addition, the TRIPS Agreement, unlike CBD or ITPGR, does not acknowledge the essential role of women in rural communities in conserving biodiversity. It does not make any provision to ensure the sharing of benefits from technology and innovation, or require any prior informed consent of the people (primarily women) whose knowledge is tapped for technological innovation.

Responses from civil society and Southern governments

Sustained pressure is being applied on the TRIPS Council by civil society in developing countries (including India, Brazil, China, Cuba, Dominican Republic, Ecuador, Pakistan, Thailand, Venezuela, Zambia, and Zimbabwe) to include additional clauses to the TRIPS Agreement. These are intended to ensure that an applicant for a patent relating to biological materials or indigenous knowledge shall provide disclosure of the source and country of origin of the biological resources and of the indigenous knowledge used in the invention. The applicant would also have to provide evidence of prior informed consent, and of fair and equitable benefit sharing under the relevant national regimes.

These countries are also pressing for an international regime which would grant protection to indigenous knowledge. Due to opposition from developed countries, particularly the USA, no action has been taken on these proposals. On the contrary, developed countries are advocating a 'TRIPS-plus' approach. The USA and EU have been putting pressure on weaker countries to get them to accept IPR regimes even in excess of what the WTO demands. There are a number of bilateral or regional treaties between developed and developing countries with more stringent rules than those provided under TRIPS.

The TRIPS Agreement does not specify what constitutes an 'effective' *sui generis* system. Taking account of this flexibility, a few countries have developed their own laws, reflecting the combined obligations of the CBD and TRIPS. The 'Protection of Plant Varieties and Farmers' Rights Act of India' is one such example. It balances farmers' and breeders' rights, recognises farmer varieties, and provides for monetary compensation for their use by breeders. The 'Model Law for the Protection of the Rights of Local Communities, Farmers and Breeders, and for Regulation of Access to Biological Resources', developed by the Organisation of African Unity (OAU), is a law which recognises the contribution made by farming communities to developing and maintaining bio resources. However, the developed countries are discouraging these efforts. TRIPS does not require countries to adopt UPOV as their *sui generis* system, yet there are bilateral pressures by developed

countries on poor countries to join UPOV. For instance, the 'EU–Bangladesh Trade and Aid Agreement of 1999' requires Bangladesh to 'make every effort' to join UPOV.

Impact on biodiversity, gender relations, and communities

Biodiversity is the basis of food and livelihood as well as human and animal health for poor and marginalised communities. To alter the dynamics of control and usage of biodiversity through IPR rules will further impoverish and marginalise local communities, and women will be disadvantaged, in terms of both their economic and decision-making roles.

The case of the Canadian farmer Percy Schmeiser and his dispute with Monsanto over an alleged violation of IPR shows the way in which IPR regimes are being implemented by corporations to establish monopolies. Monsanto sued Schmeiser for huge damages for violating its patent on 'Roundup Ready' canola, after specimens of the proprietary canola were found on Schmeiser's property. Canola is a cross-pollinating crop, so the likely source of the offending canola was pollen from a nearby 'Roundup Ready' field, but the case demonstrates the extent to which multinational companies will go to establish monopolies on bio-resources. Such actions would have grave consequences in developing countries, since denying rights over vital resources would affect the community's ability to survive.

Commercial interests that target bio-resources on a large scale for the market will threaten the bio-resource base, and the knowledge base associated with it The impact on women, and through them families, will be immediate. There is a steady depletion of rare medicinal flora from the hill regions, because of collections being conducted by pharmaceutical companies.

A sub-species of *Taxus baccata*, the Himalayan Yew tree in the Himalayan region, is facing near extinction as a consequence of over-exploitation for its cancer-curing properties. Large areas of the Kumaon and Garhwal Himalayas in India have been stripped of medicinal plants by head loaders collecting for foreign and Indian companies. This devastation of flora means that women lose the resources they need for use in home remedies to treat their families and their livestock (Sahai 1996).

Patents on seeds would limit women's ability to breed new, locally adapted varieties for food, healing, and rituals. This would strike at nutritional security for families and also at the socio-cultural identity of communities, as women have bred varieties integral to local food habits and cultural and religious practices.

When patents are permitted, there is currently no requirement for disclosing the source of the plant material, nor the key information lead for the claimed 'invention': that is, the indigenous knowledge of the characteristics, say of the particular medicinal plant. Bio-piracy constitutes a misappropriation of the intellectual property of local communities. In the case of the patent on turmeric, or *neem*, the knowledge of the wound-healing property or the bactericidal property of the respective plants was the basis of the 'invention' that was granted a patent by the US Patent and Trademark Office. The consequences could be twofold. Exercise of the patent in India could lead to corporate control over wound-healing or antiseptic products derived from turmeric and neem. On the other hand, if such products had the potential for export to the USA, such an opportunity could be denied, because the existing US patent could be used to block any imports.

Whether in the field of medicinal plants or in agriculture, women will be excluded from the decision-making process. They will have less say in what will be planted in the field, because seed availability will increasingly shift to crops with a single dominant trait. Women are likely to have fewer options and less flexibility to use bio-resources for multiple uses. Since participation in the cash economy to make up the loss in these sectors will either not be possible for women or will place additional burdens on them, it is also likely that the ensuing deprivations will become permanent (GTZ 2001).

The way ahead

The only way to fully ensure a fair deal for communities in developing countries is to remove biodiversity from TRIPS altogether. Since achieving this ambitious goal may take more time than the mandated review period allows, one way might be to secure a five-year suspension of the implementation of Article 27.3(b), so that developing countries may sort out their strategies. In any case, developing countries must at least ensure that there is no strengthening of the TRIPS Agreement, as some developed countries are trying to do through bilateral treaties.

It is important to develop alternatives to UPOV. This direction must be strengthened in order to secure the interests of small farmers, women, and rural communities. A non-UPOV treaty on IPR regimes for seeds should seek to do the following, among other things:

- Provide reliable, good-quality seeds to small and large farmers.
- Maintain genetic diversity in the field.
- Acknowledge the enormous contribution of rural and tribal women to the identification, maintenance, and refinement of germplasm.
- Emphasise that the countries of the tropics are germplasm-owning countries and the primary source of agricultural varieties.
- Develop a system wherein farmers and breeders have recognition and rights

accruing from their respective contributions to the creation of new varieties.

The other approach could be to negotiate at the international level for establishing the primacy of CBD over TRIPS. Article 22 of the CBD states: 'The provisions of this Convention shall not affect the rights and obligations of any Contracting Party deriving from any existing international agreement, *except where the exercise of those rights and obligations would cause a serious damage or threat to biological diversity*' [emphasis added] (CBD 1992).

It is clear that the implementation of TRIPS is detrimental to the health of biological diversity, and therefore its implementation must be made subservient to the conditions of the CBD. There is also a large body of opinion that IPRs should not be regulated under the WTO at all. Refining the jurisdiction of TRIPS would be part of a more fundamental reassessment of whether trade policy instruments governing market access should determine national intellectual property regimes.

Dr Suman Sahai is the Convenor of Gene Campaign, based in New Delhi. She has published extensively in science and policy issues related to food security. She is a member of several national policy forums on research and education, international trade, biodiversity and environment, rural development, biotechnology and bio ethics and intellectual property rights.
mail@genecampaign.org /genecamp@vsnl.com
http://www.genecampaign.org

References

Balakrishna, P. (2000) 'Moving Towards Trade Negotiations of WTO and its Implications on Environment and Biodiversity', paper presented at the Training Seminar on 'WTO, UNCTAD and Regionalism: Implications for the Private and Public Sectors in South Asia', Law and Society Trust, Colombo.

Conventional on Biological Diversity (1992) www.biodiv.org/convention/article.asp

Gaia Foundation – GRAIN (1998) 'Ten reasons not to join UPOV', *Global Trade and Biodiversity in Conflict*, Vol. 2.

Gene Campaign and CEAD (1998) 'Convention of Farmers and Breeders (CoFaB)', a draft treaty presented as an alternative to UPOV, New Delhi.

GTZ (Deutsche Gesellschaft für Technische Zusammenarbeit GmbH) (2001) 'Gender Relations and Biodiversity', Issue Papers BIODIV, www.gtz.de/biodiv.

GTZ (Deutsche Gesellschaft für Technische Zusammenarbeit GmbH) (2002) 'Local Knowledge of Conserving Biodiversity from a Gender Perspective', Project Papers BIODIV, www.flora.org.pe.

Krishna, S. (1998) 'Gender and bio diversity management', in M.S. Swaminathan (ed.). *Gender Dimensions in Biodiversity Management*, Konark, New Delhi.

Leskien, D. and M. Flitner (1997) 'Intellectual property rights and plant genetic resource: options for a *sui generis* system', *Issues in Genetic Resource 6*, IPGRI, Rome.

Mulvany, P. (1999) 'TRIPs, Biodiversity and Commonwealth Countries: Capacity building priorities for the 1999 review of TRIPs Article 27.3 (b)'. Paper prepared for Commonwealth Secretariat and Quaker Peace and Service, Geneva.

NGO Women's Forum, Germany and Working Group 'Women' in the Forum Environment and Development (2002)

'Social, Economic and Environmental Sustainability from a Gender Perspective', WIDE Position Paper, www.nro-frauenforun.de.

Rani, M.G. and M. S. Swaminathan (1998) 'Biodiversity in India: Heritage and management', in Swaminathan (ed.) *Gender Dimensions in Biodiversity Management*, Konark, New Delhi.

Sahai, S. (1996) 'How do we protect our genetic resources?', *Economic and Political Weekly*, New Delhi.

Sahai, S. (2000) 'GATT/WTO and the TRIPS Agreement: a South Asia perspective', *South Asia Economic Journal*, 1 (2): 25–41.

Sahai, S. (2001) 'The TRIPS Agreement: Implications for developing countries'. Paper presented at 'Workshop on Threats to Indian Agriculture Posed by the WTO Regime', Hyderabad.

Sahai, S. (2002a) 'India's plant variety protection and farmer's right legislation', in P. Drahos and R. Mayne (eds.) *Global Intellectual Property Rights*, Basingstoke: Palgrave Macmillan

Sahai, S. (2002b) 'The TRIPS Agreement: Implications for farmer's rights and food security'. Paper presented at 'Asia Pacific Conference on Food Security' CIROAP Meeting, Hong Kong.

Sahai, S. (2003) 'Importance of indigenous knowledge', *Indian Journal of Traditional Knowledge*, 2(1): 11–14.

Sreenivasan, G. and J. Christie (2002) 'Intellectual Property, Biodiversity and the Right of the Poor', Canadian Council for International Co-operation Trade and Poverty Series, Paper 3.

Women, trade, and migration

Don Flynn and Eleonore Kofman

The impact of modern trade policies on the position of women across the world has produced a growing literature in recent years. This has largely concentrated on analyses of the impact on women of privatisation and trade liberalisation during the course of the past two decades. There has been increased interest on the part of the OECD, World Bank, and International Organization for Migration, and international NGOs in the relationship between trade and migration. However, there has to date been very little discussion of gender issues in relation to this nexus. In this article we will look at the effect on women of trade liberalisation policies and migration.

There are two aspects to the current debate on women, trade, and migration. The first concerns the unfavourable terms of trade between North and South which have contributed to pressure on women to migrate from their homelands. The second concerns measures to expand trade in services through the physical movement of persons. This is the subject of the GATS (General Agreement on Trade in Services) Mode 4 (Nielson 2002), which seeks to liberalise trade in persons to balance trade in services, goods, and capital. For the moment this primarily concerns highly skilled workers and those employed in transnational corporations, but there has been pressure from a number of developing countries to include less skilled workers.

Mode 4 covers the temporary movement of employees from foreign companies operating in countries where they have no permanent presence. Although there is no provision within GATS to limit eligibility to workers who hold a particular range of qualifications, in practice many developed countries have restricted Mode 4 to investment-related movements. In negotiations, developing countries have favoured a wider scope for Mode 4 movement, encompassing transport, tourism, health and care services, and contract cleaning. They see advantages in arrangements which facilitate the export of surplus labour, and they hope for gains from the transfer of income to the home country from workers abroad. The gap between the two groups of countries on these issues has remained wide, and little progress has been made in recent times in reaching common agreement.

Too often it is assumed that GATS Mode 4 is of little consequence for women. We shall argue that the prevailing global shortage of labour in reproductive sectors such as education, care, and health has considerable gender impact (Kofman 2004), but has received little attention from national and international organisations.

Gender, trade, and migratory movements

The continuing trend towards globalisation has closed down many options for progress, other than drastic restructuring to increase competitiveness in export markets. The two best-known attempts to force this issue have been the structural adjustment programmes (SAPs), favoured by the World Bank and the International Monetary Fund (IMF), and a more recent generation of free trade agreements.

The experiences of two decades have provided evidence of a bleak outcome for women resulting from both approaches. Mariama Williams (1998) has argued that the strategy of SAPs in Africa during the 1980s left women significantly worse off as dramatic cuts in social spending increased responsibilities in the provision of welfare and health care in the domestic sphere. At the same time, increased dependency on monetary incomes forced a larger number of women to seek paid employment. SAP-inspired cuts in the provision of education and training meant that the work available was invariably at the low-skill, low-pay end of the spectrum, and that economic opportunities were reduced.

Gender impact surveys have been conducted in relation to recent free trade agreements. One example is the Central America Free Trade Agreement (CAFTA) between the United States and the Central American countries. The unequal balance of power in these negotiations generally means that developing countries are required to abandon state support for key elements in their national economies, while the heavily subsidised agriculture and manufacturing of the developed partners remain untouched.

The International Gender and Trade Network (IGTN) has reported on the ways in which forced liberalisation of the agricultural sector in Central American countries will worsen levels of hunger and food insecurity, resulting in an increased burden for women as the primary carers (IGTN, n.d.). The growth of poverty in rural areas is already leading to increased migration to cities and towns for employment in the export-orientated *maquilas* factories,[1] where women are disadvantaged by exploitative and sexist working conditions. The IGTN assessment suggests that CAFTA contributes to pressures on women to join the migratory movements to the United States, which currently draw in an estimated 200,000–300,000 people a year. This study provides a relatively rare example of a link being made between trade and gender, development, and migration.

The International Organisation for Migration (IOM) estimates that almost half of the world's 175 million migrants are women (IOM 2003). Historically a large proportion of female migrants will have travelled as the spouses of male migrants, or other family dependants and this has been one of the reasons for the higher percentage of female migrants in developed regions. Today 50.9 per cent of migrants in the developed world are women, compared with 45.7 per cent in the less developed world (Zlotnik 2003). Women are increasingly migrating as workers themselves, and in some countries this trend is growing dramatically. Among Sri Lankan migrants, for example, the proportion of women rose from 33 per cent in 1986 to 65 per cent in 1999 (IOM 2003). Some have professional qualifications which allow them to benefit from expanding opportunities for skilled migration (Kofman 2000); others will be reliant on the niches opening up in the service sector for domestic workers, carers, cleaners, and caterers.

These new job areas are the product of changing lifestyles in developed countries, but they can lead to the de-skilling of large numbers of women (McKay 2002; Parrenas 2001; Phizacklea 2003). In countries such as Canada, for example, the 'Live-in Care Giver Program' requires workers with high educational standards, but then locks them into employment with a specific employer for two years, during which time it is very difficult for them to maintain or improve their skills. In this way many Filipina workers have become de-skilled (McKay 2002; Stasiulis and Bakan 2003).

Current research on the conditions and processes of migration seeks to understand the connections between sending and receiving countries within the global economy. According to Sassen (2000), globalisation has produced a set of dynamics in which women are playing a critical role, as global cities in developed countries witness the return of 'serving classes' composed largely of migrant women (2000: 510). She analyses the relationship between 'low-income individuals, who are represented as a burden rather than a resource' and 'significant sources for profit and government revenue enhancement' (506). Debt and debt servicing, for example, have become a systemic feature of the developing world since the 1980s. Subsequent cut-backs in social programmes have precipitated the search for employment overseas.

Policy makers have displayed a growing interest in the idea of migrants as a force for development. Economic progress can be promoted through migrant workers' remittances. In 2003 the World Bank estimated the global value of cash returned to countries of origin by overseas worker communities to be in excess of US$ 90 billion (DFID/World Bank 2003:3). In contrast to cash flows from foreign direct and portfolio investment, remittances are highly stable over time, and in fact even increase in response to economic crises. There is also substantial evidence linking remittances to poverty reduction, although these remittances may increase inequalities between households with relatives abroad and those without (Boswell and Crisp 2004).

In India, for example, remittances totalled $US 7.6 billion, almost three times more than net investment flows and almost as much as the contribution of the textile and clothing industry (Nielson 2002). In the Philippines, overseas Filipino workers (OFWs) are now considered the new heroes as, for example, they brought in $US 6.23 billion in remittances in 2000, enough to fill the gap in shortfalls in revenue and balance of payments. The largest proportion (53 per cent) was sent back from the USA, but other countries in Asia (Korea, Japan, Hong Kong, and Singapore) and now the UK (2 per cent) were also significant. The Philippines Overseas Employment Administration, established in 1982, organises and oversees the export of nurses and maids. In 2000, 70 per cent – 178,323 out of 253,030 – OFWs were women (Philippine Overseas Employment Administration 2000). An equally high percentage were women in the professional and technical category.

Research suggests that men and women exhibit different remittance behaviour, with men favouring the purchase of consumer items such as televisions and cars from the money sent home, while women choose health care, food, and schooling. (DFID/World Bank 2003: 9). Some scholars have suggested the possibility that, beyond the household, female migrant remittances have a dynamic effect on traditional gender roles (Asian Studies conference 2004). As remitters, women can acquire new status and authority, giving directions on the allocation of resources to projects within the family and the community. Women in remittance-wealthy families can escape domestic work by hiring maids and servants from poorer households.

If migration appears to offer the possibility of a transformation of the position of women, while also threatening vulnerable groups, the question is whether policies can be pursued which enhance the prospect of the former, while diminishing the danger of the latter.

Gendered aspects of GATS and immigration policies

In a set of recommendations emanating from a seminar in Jakarta in December 2003, UN Development for Women (UNIFEM) called for action on 'recognising, protecting and empowering women migrant workers in Asia' (UNIFEM 2003). This action would involve the 'main-streaming of gender concerns in migration into national and regional poverty reduction policies and programmes', and the promotion of 'collaboration within and between countries of origin and employment, including bilateral and multi-lateral agreements to protect migrant workers'.

In the past decade there has been an expansion of skilled labour to meet shortages in IT, education, and health services and to support production, sales, and servicing in transnational corporations. Temporary, short-term movements have been increasing rapidly in these sectors. A trade agreement on the 'movement of persons' has been concluded by NAFTA (Chapter 6) between Mexico, Canada, and the United States.

The movement of persons has also been taken up by the WTO in its General Agreement on Trade in Services (GATS), which divides trade in services into four modes of supply. Mode 4 refers to the supply of services via the presence of natural persons, whereas Mode 3 refers to the more prevalent supply of services via commercial flows. Mode 4 is intended for temporary or non-permanent movements in fulfilment of contracts, ranging from several weeks to 3–5 years, for a specific purpose and confined to a particular sector rather than within a general programme of migration.

The liberalisation of capital and supply of services (Mode 3) works in favour of developed countries. India, perceiving that there were advantages for developing countries issuing from the liberalisation of labour, exported large numbers of engineers, IT specialists, and health workers. For many

countries, as we have seen, remittances from workers often constitute far larger sums than net direct investment. Thus some developing countries have indicated that their willingness to negotiate in the WTO on Mode 3 investment will depend on progress in Mode 4 discussions (Nielson 2002).

While some developing countries may be pushing for greater opening up of markets, the increasing dependence of developed countries on foreign nurses raises ethical issues about recruitment. Emigration of professional workers is likely to undermine the delivery of education and health services in many developing countries. African countries, such as Zambia, are particularly concerned about loss of skilled migrants, who frequently prolong their stay abroad. Although some countries such as the Philippines virtually train nurses for export, others, such as South Africa and countries in the Caribbean, have reached an agreement with the UK government not to recruit nurses. However, although the National Health Service may not be recruiting, private agencies still do.

Wages and conditions which temporary foreign workers receive are also issues for trade unions. Fifty WTO members have included in their stipulation for Mode 4 that conditions should guarantee wages comparative with nationals. The ILO Constitution includes the principle of equal pay for work of equal value (Boswell and Crisp 2004). However, complexities of labour contracting in fields where workers are paid home-country levels plus allowances make this a difficult area to police. Problems are known to exist, for example, in sectors such as hospitality services and agriculture, where a workforce containing large numbers of women is recruited by agencies based in the sending countries. To women placed on short-term contracts during periods of high seasonal demand, wages will often be paid in local currency into bank accounts in the countries of origin, at levels below the national minimal rates in the labour-using countries.

Although developing countries would like GATS Mode 4 to be extended to less-skilled jobs, developed countries are reluctant to recognise the necessity of labour in these sectors. Very few countries acknowledge the vital work being undertaken by the most feminised jobs, especially in the private domestic sector (Anderson 2000) and in care. Countries in Mediterranean Europe have established quotas for domestic labour (Anderson 2000), while several Asian countries (Yamanaka and Piper 2003) recruit large numbers of women for this purpose. Nevertheless, the levels often remain insufficient to meet demand for changing welfare regimes where emphasis is increasingly placed on privatised provision (Mitchell et al. 2003).

The informalisation of employment in many sectors means that, although workers may not be eligible for work permits, demand is buoyant. Although GATS may open up some legal routes, these will be limited, and largely restricted to skilled jobs. When legal options are tightly constrained, people resort to routes managed by criminals involved in trafficking and smuggling activities (Boswell and Crisp 2004). The over-representation of female workers in the informal service sector means that women are drawn into labour-smuggling networks in disproportionate numbers.

Even after arrival in the destination country, female migrants are disempowered by many factors. Absence of labour protection laws, cultures of sexism, low wages, poor working conditions, and lack of job security create vulnerability and opportunities for gross exploitation.[2] Networks of support from groups acting in solidarity can provide protection from the worst of these dangers. An example of a group of female migrants which has been able to mobilise such resources is the 'Kalayaan' network, supporting the rights of domestic workers. Based in London, Kalayaan, an organisation with predominantly, though not exclusively, Filipina membership, has links with the Europe-wide social service and workers' rights organisation, 'Solidar'.[3]

Despite the enormous difficulties created by restrictive immigration regimes and abusive employers, migration can provide a route towards empowerment and emancipation for many women (Kofman et al. 2000; Parrenas 2001). Migration can confer on women recognition of their major contribution to family survival, or enable them to escape from marital difficulties (Phizacklea 2003). As it is expected that the migration of women will continue to grow as trade liberalisation develops in the coming years, we need to pursue more vigorously the human-rights protections which are available in a number of the more widely ratified treaties.[4] There is, as well, the International Convention on the Protection of the Rights of All Migrant Workers and Members of Their Families (Migrant Workers' Convention), which entered into force on 1 July 2003 (Sattherwaite 2004).

Possible ways forward

Despite their engagement with issues of female labour migration, NGOs, scholars, and international agencies have yet to develop assessments on the relationship of this migration with trade policy. The UNIFEM Jakarta recommendations, comprehensive in other respects, do not sustain detailed reflection on the links between globalisation, trade, and migration. While a growing number of studies have begun to sketch out terrain in which further work might take place (Ghosh 1997; Simmons 1996), a rigorous overview of gender, trade, and migration issues has yet to be developed.

Some sense of what might become possible in developing this overview can be seen in the sustainability impact assessment (SIA) approach developed by the Commission of the European Union (EU). The SIA methodology is designed to provide information on the possible impacts of trade policy to ensure that the final decisions are the optimal ones. Engagement with all stakeholders affected by the trade regime is imperative within the SIA schema.

Examples of SIAs conducted to date include the economic partnership agreements (EPAs) with the African, Caribbean, and Pacific (ACP) countries in the Cotonou agreement (CEC 2003). Immigration in a variety of contexts is discussed in these studies, but the participation of women and their distinct role in migratory movements is not profiled to any significant extent.

If SIAs represent the cutting edge of trade policy evaluation at the present time, they reveal something of the dilemma for those concerned with gender issues. An analysis of the issues outlined by feminist advocates on trade issues in IGTN circles, and drawing on available data on female migration, is scarcely represented in policy formulation by intergovernment institutions.

There is scope for an expansion of co-operation between groups of trade and immigration rights activists in the period ahead. The area most likely for collaboration in the immediate future is that of remittances. Measures are needed to facilitate low-cost money transfers, and to encourage household expenditures which promote welfare and employment gains, as opposed to non-productive consumption, in the sending countries. Forums do exist in which the interests of women migrants can be repre-sented in policy formulation. The International Gender and Trade Network was set up in 1999 following the collapse of WTO talks in Seattle and has been part of a greater engagement with the WTO and UNCTAD (United Nations Conference on Trade and Development). Trade liberalisation of goods, services, and people touches upon many economic and social issues and has a differ-ential impact on women and men as migrants. Gender issues as they affect migrant workers have to be taken seriously, as new agree-ments are being reached on CAFTA and GATS, the latter due to be agreed in 2005.

Don Flynn is policy officer of the London-based Joint Council for the Welfare of Immigrants (JCWI). He is active in NGO networks promoting the rights of migrants in the UK and Europe. Eleonore Kofman is Professor of Human Geography at Nottingham Trent University. She is co-author of Gender and International Migration in Europe: Employment, welfare and politics (Routledge, 2000).
don@jcwi.org.uk; eleonore.kofman@ntu.ac.uk

Notes

1 The *maquila* programme originated in Mexico. It allows foreign companies to operate with special exemptions on normal customs regulations with regard to the importation of capital equipment. All the products of a *maquiladora* corporation are required to be exported.

2 Evidence given by 'Tatiana Volkova' (assumed name), a key witness in the trial of the organisers of a prostitution ring in London in March 2004, provides a not untypical account of the ways in which the dynamics of low-paid and insecure employment expose many female migrants to the menaces of organised crime (*Daily Mirror*, 22 March 2004)

3 www.solidar.org.

4 These include CEDAW (ratified by 174 countries), the International Covenant on Civil and Political Rights (151 countries), the Covenant on Economic, Social and Cultural Rights (148 countries), and the Convention on the Elimination of All Forms of Racial Discrimination (174 countries).

References

Anderson, B. (2000) *Doing the Dirty Work? The global politics of domestic labour*, London: Zed.

Asian Studies Japan Conference (2004) Digest of papers. Ichigaya campus of Sophia University, 2004.

Boswell, C. and J. Crisp (2004) 'Poverty, International Migration and Asylum, Policy Brief no. 8', Helsinki: World Institute for Development Economics Research of UN University.

Commission of the European Communities (CEC) (2003) 'Sustainability Impact Assessment (SIA) of the trade negotiations of the EU–ACP Economic Partnership Agreements; Working draft 01', October 2003, PriceWaterhouse Cooper, consultants.

DFID/World Bank (2003) 'International Conference on Migrant Remittances: Report and Conclusions', London.

Ghosh, B. (1997) *Gains from Global Linkages: Trade in services and movements of persons*, New York: St. Martin's Press.

IGTN, 'Gender Impacts of CAFTA', www.igtn.org, n.d.

IOM (2003) 'World Migration 2003: Managing Migration – Challenges and responses for people on the move', Geneva, Textbox 1.1.

Kofman, E., A. Phizacklea, P. Raghuram, and R. Sales (2000) *Gender and International Migration in Europe*, London: Routledge.

Kofman, E. (2004) 'Gender and global migrations: Diversity and stratification', *International Feminist Journal of Politics*, 6, forthcoming.

McKay, D. (2002) 'Filipina Identities: Geographies of social integration/exclusion in the Canadian metropolis', Vancouver Centre of Excellence Working Paper Series 01-18.

Mitchell, K., S. Marston, and C. Katz (2003) 'Introduction: life's work: an introduction, review and critique', *Antipode* 35(3): 415–42.

Nielson, Julia (2002) 'Service providers on the move: labour mobility and the WTO General Agreement on Trade in Services', Evian Group Compendium, 2002.

OECD–World Bank–IOM (2003) 'International Seminar on Trade and Migration 12–14 November', ICFTU Report.

Parrenas, R. (2001) *Servants of Globalization*, Stanford: Stanford University Press.

Philippine Overseas Employment Administration (2000) 'Deployed New Hire Landbased Workers by Sex 1992–2002'. Available at www.poea.gov.ph/html/statistics.html

Phizacklea, A. (2003) 'Transnationalism, gender and global workers' in Morokvasic and Shinozaki (eds.) *Crossing Borders and Shifting Boundaries. Vol 1 Gender on the Move*, Opladen: Leske and Budrich.

Sassen, S. (2000) 'Countergeographies of globalisation: the feminisation of survival', *Journal of International Affairs* 53 (2): 503–24.

Sattherthwaite, M. (2004) 'Women migrants' rights under international human rights law', *Feminist Review* 77.

Simmons, A. (ed.) (1996) 'International Migration, Refugee Flows and Human Rights: The Impact of Trade and Restructuring', New York: The Centre for Migration Studies.

Stasiulis, D. and A. Bakan, (2003) *Renegotiating Citizenship. Migrant women in Canada and the global system*, Hampshire and New York: Palgrave.

Status of Women Canada (2003) *Gender and International Trade: an annotated bibliography*, Ottawa.

INIFEM (2003) 'The Jakarta Recommendations for Action on Recognizing, Protecting and Empowering Women Migrant Workers in Asia', from the Regional Workshop on Protecting Women Migrant Workers, 9–11 December 2003, Jakarta. Available at www.unifem-eseasia.org/projects/migrant/recommendations.htm

Williams, Mariama (1998) *Structural Adjustment, Trade Liberalisation and Economic and Social Rights*, UNESCO.

Yamanaka, K. and N. Piper (2003) 'An Introductory Overview', *Asian and Pacific Migration Journal* 12(2): 1–19.

Zlotnik, H. (2003) 'The global dimensions of female migration', *Migration Information Source*, March.

Gender, the Doha Development Agenda, and the post-Cancun trade negotiations

Mariama Williams

The intensification of trade liberalisation has increasingly led women's organisations and other civil society groups to pay close attention to the impact of trade liberalisation on economic and social development. At the last Ministerial meeting of the WTO in Cancun, gender and trade advocates developed empirical and policy-oriented positions on the WTO trade agenda. Though critical of the previous Doha Development Agenda (DDA) of 2001, the groups are concerned that even its minimal pro-development stance might be reduced in the post-Cancun period leading up to the next meeting in Hong Kong. This would be detrimental to economic development and to the well-being of men and women in the South.

Gender and trade liberalisation: an overview

After the spectacular failures of two WTO Ministerial Conferences in Seattle (1999) and Cancun (2003) over the same set of issues, promotion of trade liberalisation as the engine of growth and development is clearly under attack. The failures have revolved around the clash of expectations and ambitions of developing and developed countries (Palley 2004). The developing countries had high ambitions for agricultural liberalisation, which they identified as the critical ingredient for development. However, the powerful countries had high ambitions for non-agricultural market access.

Undeniably, trade liberalisation generates changes in the domestic economy and in economic and social development. Conventional wisdom presupposes that the effects are always unambiguously positive for development as well as for poverty reduction within and across countries. Conventional wisdom also assumes that the impacts of trade liberalisation are beneficial to men and women – or at least gender-neutral.

However, trade liberalisation has specific economic, political, and social effects, which can worsen the already unequal situation of women in terms of access to land, credit, training, technology, and domestic and household responsibilities. This raises the issue of how women and men are faring under changes in trade-policy regimes oriented towards the reduction and elimination of import barriers.

Current research points to a two-way relationship between trade liberalisation and gender: trade liberalisation can increase or decrease gender inequality, and gender inequality can prevent trade liberalisation from achieving the desired results. A government may enact a particular trade reform measure, thinking that it will increase trade, without considering the constraints operating on the dominant groups in each sector, and how these affect responses to policy change.

Research on agriculture (Baden 1998, Madeley 2000, and Quisumbing *et al.* 1995) demonstrates this experience in some African countries. In Uganda, for example, trade-liberalisation policies led to the closing of local state trading enterprise (STE) depots. Although lack of access to the STEs affected both men and women, it had a disproportionately detrimental effect on women (Sengendo and Tumushabe 2002). Due to their greater mobility, men were able to travel outside their villages to sell products, whereas women were forced to sell products closer to home at lower prices. Trade liberalisation also caused a switch to export crops, which created land speculation and loss of common property resources. Women as a group have a higher dependence on common property than men.

Trade liberalisation can stimulate increased employment for some groups of women and men. It can provide opportunities for entrepreneurship and sustainable liveli-hoods, access to resources and technology, and to an overseas market. But trade liberalisation can also result in reduced access to affordable food, shelter, and basic services. Women farmers and entrepreneurs, comprising a large proportion of small and medium-sized enterprise holders (SMEs), may actually lose livelihoods and markets through competition with highly subsidised goods produced in developed countries. They may also be unfavourably affected by changes in investment regimes.

The Uruguay round of trade agreements (1986–1994) was the most comprehensive set of negotiations in the multilateral trading system. However, since the emergence of the WTO in 1995, its activities have raised concerns about the impact of trade liberalisation on social and environmental dimensions of economic development in the South.

The debates

The WTO Ministerial meetings, which have so far occurred on average every two years (Singapore 1996, Geneva 1998, Seattle 1999, and Doha 2001), are forums for compre-hensive reviews and reforms of trade rules. The outcomes of these deliberations are usually issued in the form of a Ministerial Declaration and accompanying annexes. While the Ministerials are not the only source of WTO rule making, they are the WTO's most public and high-level events. Thus they have been the focus of a great deal of interest, agitation, and monitoring by civil society.

The Fourth Ministerial Meeting of the World Trade Organisation, in Doha, Qatar, in 2001, produced the Doha Declaration. This seemed to promise everything that was not addressed in previous rounds. In attempting to make development the centre-piece of WTO trade negotiations, the Doha Development Agenda (DDA) placed for discussion the resolution of more than 80 implementation issues arising from developing countries' attempt to follow through on the commitments made in the Uruguay Round Agreements (URA). Ultimately, many developing countries argued that some of the provisions of the URA are unfair, that they are biased against them, and that they require extensive resources, which they can least afford.

The DDA included a declaration that the Trade-Related Aspects of Intellectual Property Rights (TRIPS) agreement does not prevent governments from fulfilling their public-health responsibilities. Hence, govern-ments, in the public interest, can authorise the production of patented products as medicines without the permission of the patent holder.[2] The DDA also promised 'substantial improvement on market access, the phasing out of all forms of export subsidy, and substantial reduction in domestic support' (Ministerial Declaration, 2001, para 13). This would help to reduce the dumping of subsidised food exports from the EU and the USA in developing countries. Doha further promised that non-trade concerns such as animal welfare, biodiversity protection, employment, environment, food security, and welfare would be taken into account for the first time in the agricultural negotiations.

The Doha agenda further extended the WTO's scope into domestic regulatory areas by including competition policy, government procurement, investment, and trade facilitation within the negotiating framework. These four issues are also known as 'the Singapore Issues'. Although developing countries, as a group, were opposed to the launching of negotiation on these issues, proponents argued that the issues were ripe for negotiations. The Doha Ministerial, however, ruled that the four issues could be considered for negotiations only by 'explicit consensus' of all Members of the WTO at the Fifth (Cancun) Ministerial (paras 20, 23, 26 and 27, Ministerial Declaration November 14, 2001).

Contrary interpretations of this were not resolved in Geneva by the time of the Cancun meeting. The matter thus became the critical stumbling block in reaching consensus on a Ministerial Declaration at Cancun and it substantially contributed to the failure of that meeting. As a result of the impasse, the timeline for ending negotiations on the DDA, which was due to conclude in 2005, has to be shifted to possibly 2006–2007. Extension of the Doha Round deadline presents opportunities and challenges for down-scaling the trade-liberalisation agenda of the rich countries and reducing social inequities linked to it. It would make room for gendered social and environmental assessments of the Uruguay Round of Trade Agreements.

These are the critical expectations overshadowing the proposed sixth WTO Ministerial, currently set for Hong Kong in 2005. As with Cancun, these expectations revolve around reviving the Doha Development Round. But what are the key aspects and assumptions of the DDA? How will it affect gender equality? And how can gender and trade advocates make gains in enhancing gender equality and social development effects of future trade negotiations?

The gender dimensions of trade from Uruguay, to Doha and Cancun

Thus far multilateral trade negotiations have pursued trade liberalisation through market access and reduction of restrictions on the movement of goods and services across borders, without attention to impacts on different sectors of an economy. Three broad areas of the Cancun negotiations have implications for gender dynamics and women's economic and social position. These are agriculture, services, and the 'Singapore Issues'.

Agreement on Agriculture (AOA)
The focus of agricultural liberalisation is on reducing protection through promoting market access and attacking export (competition) subsidy and domestic support. It relies on the replacement of restrictions such as import quotas and licensing with tariff equivalents. However, more often than not, tariffication results in high levels of protection, which hinder developing countries' exports into developed countries' markets.

Trade liberalisation tends to generate cheap agricultural products, which may result in lower farm-gate prices. It is also accompanied by increased competition with foreign imports. Overall the combination of these factors, plus the removal of subsidies in developing countries, may lead both to increased income (from the export sector) and to decreased income (because of the import-competing sectors). Many women and their families are left worse off than before the liberalisation policy. As noted by Jepkerich Too-Yego (cited in Madeley 2000), this has definitely been the case in Kenya, where increased food imports and dumping, coupled with an increase in the price of farm input, have left women worse off than they were in 1981. Many poor farmers, the poorest of whom are women, cannot afford adequate chemicals, fertiliser, and other farm inputs.

The AOA, negotiated under the Uruguay Round, attempted to impose conditions on domestic subsidy and support for agricultural production. However, the final outcome was disproportionate in that the rich countries were able to protect their agriculture under the so-called 'peace clause'.

In recent negotiations, developing countries have tried to call for their own set of special boxes – the 'development box' and the 'food security box'. However, these became discussions on 'strategic products' such as cotton, sugar, and dairy products, and Special Safeguard Mechanisms (SSMs), which would allow a country to raise tariffs if import volume were to rise above a certain level, or if prices fell too drastically. Thus, the SSMs would ensure a certain amount of protection (especially against dumping) to farmers in developing countries.

Post-URA, agricultural negotiations in the WTO were to include the elimination of subsidies, improved market access, the operationalisation of Special and Differential (S&D) treatment for developing countries, and expiration of the 'peace clause'.

In Cancun, developing countries argued that the EU–US proposal would not produce significant tariff reduction on products of export interest to the South. Moreover, there was no commitment to a phase-out date for export subsidies, and the text was weak on special and differential (S&D) treatment. To add further insult to the developing countries, the widely supported 'Cotton Initiative' was summarily dismissed by the USA. This initiative, proposed by West and Central African countries, called for the elimination of US and other subsidies,[3] in order that the cotton market could be sustainable for African farmers.

The General Agreement on Trade in Services (GATS)

Both agriculture and services are new areas for comprehensive multilateral trade disciplines, and there was no significant body of rules governing cross-border trade in these areas until the Uruguay Round. Services such as water, health care, and education as well as financial and professional services have become a growing part of international trade. According to the UNDP *Human Development Report 1999*, international trade in services in 1999 was about 20 per cent of total cross-border trade and about 60 per cent of global value added as a percentage of Gross Domestic Product (GDP) and employment.[4]

As with agriculture, services liberalisation and the GATS have implications for health care and health standards, job security, and conditions of work for a large number of women and men. In addition, services liberalisation has a tremendous impact on social welfare and equity. Poor people's access to water, schooling, and affordable health care may be at risk. Reduced access to and decreased affordability of social and basic services will greatly affect women and girls because of their role in social reproduction.

It is now recognised that women are likely to be over-represented among those suffering from untreated injuries and diseases, malnutrition and hunger, illiteracy and innumeracy. Reforms of the trade in services and trade-liberalisation policies that do not take these factors into account are unlikely to benefit women in their multiple roles. With the issue of water, for example, evidence from Bolivia shows that privatisation dramatically increased its cost and reduced access by the poor. Since in many developing countries women and girls have primary responsibility for ensuring household water needs, this would have a negative impact on their daily workload. As water is critical to the day-to-day lives of families, reduced access to safe water has an impact on other social reproduction roles of women.

GATS distinguishes between how a service is provided (mode of service provision) and sets rules on how countries treat foreign service-providers. In the provision of international telephone calls and distance learning, international telephone companies and foreign universities come under 'cross-border services', or Mode I. Tourism and travel for health care comes under 'consumption abroad, Mode II'. Foreign banks and McDonald's subsidiaries are covered by 'commercial presence, Mode III', and foreign nurses, doctors, and management consultants are covered by 'temporary movement of natural persons, Mode IV'.

GATS, which seeks to eliminate 'all measures affecting trade in services',[5] is a framework agreement that provides for 'progressively higher levels of liberalisation of all services'(GATS, Article XIX). To date the GATS negotiations have been focused on the process of submitting 'requests' and 'offers' for service areas in which countries desire further liberalisation on the part of their trading partners. This would expand market access to new areas and – depending on the outcomes of the negotiations – could eliminate some of the benefits to women which had been gained as a result of the exemptions to liberalisation that had been allowed in certain sectors, and which had been appended to the agreements as 'schedules' by each country involved in the trading negotiations.

The Singapore Issues[6]

The formulation of a set of four 'new' issues, known as 'Singapore Issues', prompts a certain amount of controversy concerning the multilateral trade system. Part of the controversy is that these issues are usually left to the discretion of national policy makers. Binding multilateral rules in these areas may restrict governments' decisions on areas critical to national

development. They have implications for national policy designed to deal with historical social injustice, as well as the growth and nurturing of vulnerable groups and sectors. It is therefore important to highlight how the Singapore issues could affect men and women in the economy.

Competition policy

Competition policy is the set of laws and regulations designed to maintain a fair degree of competition by eliminating restrictive business practices by private enterprises (UNDP 2003). Developing countries are generally opposed to the Multilateral Framework for Competition Policy (MFCP), which they believe provides greater market access for EU and OECD firms in developing countries and is inimical to their own local development needs. These countries also cite the fact that there are already existing multilateral rules to deal with restrictive business practices.

Women, disadvantaged minorities, and other owners and operators of small and medium-sized enterprises (SMEs) in developing countries are often under-capitalised. An MFCP is likely to reduce the support of national industrial policy in favour of SMEs and local capital, as part of sustainable and gender-equalising economic development. An MFCP is likely to have an adverse effect on government-mandated practices such as affirmative action for SMEs, especially women-owned businesses. SMEs cannot compete with the unregulated presence of transnational corporations from developed countries.[7]

Government procurement

Government procurement refers to the purchasing of intermediate goods and services by national, municipal, and local government. These goods and services are purchased for physical infrastructure, defence equipment, public good, and government administration (UNDP 2003).

The current debate on the 'government procurement agreement' is focused on 'transparency', including publication of national legislation and practices. Under the terms of the Doha mandate, government provisions which discriminate in favour of national suppliers and domestic preferences cannot be challenged. However, there are differences of opinion on all sides of the debate in relation to definitions of transparency, possible coverage (goods and services, or goods only), suppliers' rights versus government obligations, and enforcement and compliance mechanisms. Furthermore, developing countries see the introduction of transparency as a step towards government procurement coming under WTO discipline and subject to dispute settlement.

The gains of transparency to developing countries are not so clear. Proponents claim that enhanced efficiency and competition would lead to increased innovation among suppliers, reduced public expenditures (due to possible lower prices of a competitive process and likely decrease in corruption), partnership between foreign and local suppliers, good governance, and increased legal certainty. However, there is much debate about the proportion of these presumed benefits that will accrue to individual developing countries.[8]

Women entrepreneurs in SMEs may be affected by changes in procurement which would deprive them of current preferential access to government purchases. In addition, the cost of transparency must be paid for, and some budgetary items therefore must be sacrificed. Most often the trade-off would be in the social sector of the budget, which is critical for women's daily care of families and households. Finally, under a comprehensive Procurement Agreement, government loses control of purchasing as a way to stimulate local employment and markets. Some employment will definitely be lost when foreign bidders out-compete local firms, and jobs go abroad. Whether women or men are disadvantaged by the decline in

local business will depend on what sectors or firms lose out in this process, and the gendered nature of the workforce that dominates this area.

Investment

From the wide range of more than 39 proposals (of which only about four are from developing countries) presented to the WTO on the Multilateral Investment Agreement (MIA), it is clear that the main intent is to protect so-called *investors' rights*. This includes *national treatment*, whereby foreign investors must be treated as favourably as domestic investors, with no discipline on investors, and at best a benign approach to the development dimensions of investment. Developing countries are overwhelmingly opposed to an MIA in the WTO.

Much attention has been paid to gender-related impacts of 'foreign direct investment' (FDI).[9] Most studies tend to concentrate on the employment dimension, but there are a few that explore the broader questions of resource allocation and exchange-rate effects.[10] FDI has an impact on the quantity and quality of female and male employment; the nature, size, and growth potential of SMEs owned and operated by women; de-regulation of the labour market and the consequent implications for women's health and morbidity and overall long-term economic empowerment.

Trade facilitation

Trade facilitation refers to activities and practices relating to the movement, release, and clearance of goods that cross national borders (WTO 2002). This includes increasing the rules and regulations for collecting, presenting, communicating, and processing data, such as customs or licensing procedures, transport formalities, import and export procedures, insurance, and payments (WTO 2000).

Trade facilitation will involve extra budget spending. The potential loss of revenue and unexpected costs will increase stress on the budget.[11] Countries' experience implementing the WTO Agreement on Customs and Valuation includes an estimated expenditure of US$ 16.2 million in Tunisia and US$ 38.5 million in Bolivia. It is not clear to what extent trade facilitation will increase the exposure of SMEs to international trade, or impose on them additional structural disadvantages.

Towards the forthcoming Hong Kong Ministerial

Women's NGOs were very active in the many preparatory events held at Cancun, such as the International Forum on Women's Rights in Trade Agreements. While the International Forum focused on strategies for protecting women's human rights, the Association for Women's Rights and Development (AWID), Women's Edge, the Women's Environment and Development Organisation (WEDO), and the Women's International Coalition for Economic Justice (WICEJ)[12] organised an NGO Women's Caucus in Cancun.[13] The International Gender and Trade Network held daily briefing sessions for both government delegates and NGOs within the formal event.

Although women's groups have not adopted a coherent position on all the issues on the Cancun agenda, there is unity on the need to increase understanding of trade issues, and invest in gender audits of trade policy and the impact of trade liberalisation on different groups of women. Gender and trade advocates will have to formulate positions on the various sectoral provisions, as well as recommendations for trade negotiators on AOA, GATS, and the Singapore Issues.

A gender perspective on the AOA will need to elaborate a gender analysis of strategic products, food security, and special safeguard mechanisms. There needs to be a clear gender analysis of GATS, including

public services, tourism, and the differential constraints of domestic regulation on women and men. There is also need for research on the gender dimensions of the movement of natural persons, in terms of both professionals and semi- and unskilled workers, many of whom are women.

Finally, in the lead-up to the Hong Kong Ministerial, gender advocates need to develop research and policy positions on how the Singapore Issues affect women workers and entrepreneurs. There should be no expansion of the investment provision of the GATS (Mode III) to include investors' protection. More constraints imposed by GATS will limit the policy space of governments, with potentially negative implications for national development and gender equity provisions.

Mariama Williams is the Research Advisor for the International Gender and Trade Network and Co-ordinator, Political Economy and Globalisation, with responsibility for International Trade for Development Alternative With Women for a New Era (DAWN). She is also an Adjunct Associate at the Centre of Concern, Washington, DC and a Director of the Institute for Law and Economics, Kingston, Jamaica.
mariama@igtn.org

Notes

1   Important actors in bringing the attention of the international women's movement to economic issues such as structural adjustment and the debt crisis, and who are now also focusing on trade issues are: Caribbean Association for Feminist Research and Activists (CAFRA), Development Alternative with Women for a New Era, Network Women in Development Europe (WIDE), WEDO, and Women Working Worldwide. New formulations emerging out of the trade activism include the Informal Working Group on Gender and Trade (IWGGT,

Europe), the International Gender and Trade Network (IGTN), and Women's Edge.

2   This safeguard, called compulsory licensing, is justifiable when the patented medicine is essential but unavailable due to lack of supply or an unreasonably high price.

3   The US subsidy of more than $20 billion (1999–2002) to its cotton farmers guarantees them a certain price, regardless of the world price. Under this protection, US cotton production has, in turn, led to over-supply and has reduced the world market price even further.

4   It is 68 per cent of the value added for high-income countries and 38 per cent for low-income countries (Andrew Crosby and Jasmine Tacoa-Vielma (2000), 'Trade in Services and Sustainable Development: the GATS and sustainable development', *Bridges* 4(4)). www.ictsd.org/issarea/services/productd/crosbt-taco-vielma.pdf'

5   This includes government laws, policy, and regulatory and administrative rules such as grants, subsidies, licensing standards and qualifications, limitation on market access, food-safety rules, economic-needs texts and local-content provision, nationality requirements, residency requirements, technology-transfer requirement, restriction on ownership of property or land, and tax measures which affect the foreign provision of services.

6   This section draws heavily on Williams 2003b.

7   While the dominant explicit themes at Cancun are the core WTO principles of transparency, procedural fairness, and non-discrimination, market access is the underlying subtext and driving motivation.

8   At issue is the scope and definition of transparency; if too broadly defined, it will bring little benefit to development; additionally, there is the cost of implementation (logistical and bureaucratic), and finally there are bound to be significant equity and efficiency losses.

9   See for example, Braunstein (1999) and Sequino (1997).

10 These are elaborated in greater detail in Williams 2003a.

11 Pakistan, which switched to pre-shipment inspections (1995–97) before it had developed information systems and full documentation on its economy, experienced substantial under- and over-valuation by traders, resulting in a fall in revenue collection. Ultimately this put a great strain on budgetary resources (Pirzada 2002). The Philippines also experienced a similar result (Jeros, cited in UNDP 2003). On the other hand, Bolivia seems to have had an increase in revenue collection from custom reform (Gutierrez 2001).

12 The advocacy arguments and strategies for and beyond Cancun are extensively discussed in the publications of these groups and available on their various websites: www.igtn.org, www.awaid.org/cancun, www.wicej.org

13 A cursory review of the WTO NGO registration list shows that more than 18 women's organisations were formally accredited with the WTO for the Cancun meeting, including AWEPON (African Women's Policy Network); AWID; DAWN; Diverse Women for Diversity (DWD); GENTA-IGTN; GERA; HOME, Inc.; Caribbean Association for Feminist Research and Action (CAFRA); Espacio Mujeres Rumbo a Cancun; Foro Nacional de Mujeres y Politicas de Poblacion; La Coordinadora Nacional por un Milenio Feminista; Home Workers Organized for More Employment; the International Gender and Trade Network (IGTN); KULU; Korean Women

Advance Farmers (KWAFF); Mujers para el dialogo; SEWA (India); SEWA-Nepal; Women's Edge; WEDO; WICEJ; and WIDE.

References

Baden, Sally (1998) 'Gender Issues in Agricultural Liberalisation', *BRIDGE Report* No. 41. Topic paper prepared for Directorate General for Development (DGVIII) of the European Commission, Brighton: Institute of Development Studies.

Braunstein, Elise (1999) 'Engendering Foreign Direct Investment: Household structure, labor market and international mobility of capital', *World Development* 28(7):1158–72.

Gutierrez, J E. (2001) 'Customs Reform and Modernisation Program'. Presented at WTO workshop on technical assistance and capacity building in trade facilitation, 10–11 May, Geneva. www.wto.org/english/tratop_e/tradfa_e/tradefac_workshop_presentation_e.htm

Madeley, John (2000) 'Trade and hunger', in *Global Studies* No. 4, Church of Sweden, AID/Diakonai/Forum Syd.

Palley, T. (2004) 'After Cancun: Possibilities for a New North–South Grand Bargain on Trade', Washington, DC: The Open Society Institute.

Pirzada, Moeed (2002) 'Pakistan's Experience with New Trade Facilitation Measures'. Background notes for Trade and Sustainable Human Development Project, New York, UNDP.

Quisumbing, Agnes (1995) 'Gender Differences in Agricultural Productivity: A survey of empirical evidence', Washington, DC: International Food Policy Research Institute (IFPRI).

Sengendo, May C. and Godber Tumushabe (2002) 'Market Access Information Provision and Needs for Female and Male Exporters in Uganda's Horticulture and Fisheries Sectors'. Draft Research Report, Gender and Economic Reforms in Africa Phase Two Project, December, Accra, Ghana: GERA (Third World Network).

Sequino, Stephanie (1997) 'Gender Wage-inequality and Export-led Growth in South Korea and Taiwan: the effects of structural changes and economic liberalisation', Geneva: South Centre.

UNDP (2003) *Making Global Trade Work for People*, UNDP/Heinrich Boell Foundation/Rockefeller Brothers Fund/Wallace Global Fund, London: Earthscan

Williams, M. (2003a) *Gender Mainstreaming in the Multilateral Trading System*, London: Commonwealth Secretariat. www.thecommonwealth.org

Williams M. (2003b) 'Gender and the Singapore Issues: A Primer'. www.igtn.org

WTO (2000) 'Trade Facilitation Work in 2000'. http://docsonline.wto.org

WTO (2002) 'Trade Facilitation Work in 2002'. http://docsonline.wto.org

Corporate responsibility and women's employment:
the case of cashew nuts

Nazneen Kanji

We know that falling international prices and the exploitative practices of buyers and retailers have had a negative impact on the wages and working conditions of workers in developing countries. This short piece discusses an exceptional example of better practice in the cashew nut industry in Mozambique, which demonstrates that collaboration between government, companies, and civil society organisations at the national level can contribute to gender equality and sustainable development. However, in a liberalised, market-oriented environment, an analysis of potentials and constraints across the entire value chain has to inform business in developing countries, if decent wages and working conditions are to be provided. The main challenge is to find ways of strengthening business incentives at all levels for more responsible practice.

Cashew nut processing for global markets

As the cashew nut is one of the most valuable processed nuts on global commodity markets, it is also an important cash crop for farmers and has the potential to generate employment through processing and export revenue for developing countries. The world's largest producers are currently India, Vietnam, and Brazil; many countries in Africa produce smaller quantities.

Mozambique used to be the largest cashew nut producer in the 1970s, but many factors, including war and drought, inconsistent state policies and ageing trees, resulted in a decline in production (Kanji et al. 2002). In the 1990s, the privatisation of large processing factories, followed by rapid trade liberalisation, dealt a near-fatal blow to the processing sector. There are current efforts to revive both production and in-country processing, but most of the crop is exported in raw form to India, which has a processing capacity far exceeding its local production. In India, the 1990s witnessed an increase in cashew-kernel exports, with greater import liberalisation for raw nuts and a relaxation of licensing regulations for processors (Eapen et al. 2004).

With competition between producers and the recent entry of Vietnam into the world market for cashews, international prices have fallen for both raw and processed nuts. At the same time, quality requirements are increasingly applied by buyers of kernels in the USA and Europe. Both the location of 'value addition', and the buyer-driven nature of the cashew nut supply chain have had negative implications for the wages and working conditions of workers in Mozambique and India.

Wages and working conditions in cashew-processing plants

In both Mozambique and India, cashew nut processing has provided an important source of wage employment for women. The state of Kerala has the largest processing capacity in India, and there are estimated to be 400,000 women workers in the industry. In Mozambique, about 10,000 workers were employed in the industry in the early 1990s, but this number has dropped to about 2,000 at the current time (Lindberg 2001; Eapen et al. 2004).

In Kerala, with increased competition in the international market and moves towards complete liberalisation, out-sourcing of cashew processing on a commission basis (sometimes called *commission varappu*) has increased. Most public-sector factories have closed, and in private factories employers have 'seasonalised' and 'informalised' workers. The ownership of the processing sector is dominated by a few Keralan families (later generations of the men who were termed 'cashew kings' some 50 years ago). However, foreign companies also commission through agents, who may be foreign or Indian. Most workers do not earn the minimum wage, which is more likely to be earned in government-run factories than in out-sourced work. However, in all factories, men are likely to earn higher, more secure monthly salaries than women, as oven operators and supervisors, while women tend to be paid on piece rates in the shelling and peeling sections (Eapen et al. 2004).

Conditions in the factories are poor. We found that the regulations concerning ventilation and protective clothing are not followed (Eapen et al. 2004). The cashew nut shell contains a caustic liquid which burns the hands, and the coconut oil that workers use to cover their hands provides limited protection. Besides damage to the hands of women who work in the shelling section, other health problems such as back strain and reproductive complications are suffered by women who have to sit or squat in the peeling sections, or stand for long periods in the cutting sections.

In Mozambique, our study of ex-workers in Angoche, a coastal district in Nampula province, (Vijfhuizen et al. 2003a) showed that workers' livelihoods have been badly affected by factory closures and that women, more so than men, have found it difficult to find alternative sources of income. This is linked to the restrictions on women's mobility.

The new, smaller-scale factories offer piece rates, and most workers do not earn the minimum wage. However, because there are few employment opportunities, jobs in the factories are coveted; when one new factory opened in Namige, in the same province, 1,000 people turned up to apply for 70 jobs (ibid.).

In the south of Mozambique, workers in the factory that we studied started work at 4 a.m. and often worked until late afternoon in order to complete their tasks (Vijfhuizen et al. 2003b). In general, women tended to earn less than men and work longer hours, a situation which is linked to the piece rates set for the sections of the factory where women predominate, namely peeling. Men dominate in better-paid positions within the factory, including supervision and management. The implications of long hours for women are severe, given that they are primarily responsible for growing food, domestic work, and child-care. In addition, there were no maternity benefits or child-care in most factories in either country studied. By contrast, large factories in Mozambique, now closed, which provided more stable employment throughout the year also provided benefits including crèches, food, and child-care.

Better practice in employment

Although the overall findings of the study clearly show a deterioration in wages and working conditions in cashew processing in the liberalised and competitive environment, there was a single example of institutional arrangements in Mozambique where workers derived more benefits

(Vijfhuizen et al. 2003a; Kanji et al. forthcoming).

Miranda-Caju in Nampula province, Mozambique

The factory, located in the north of Mozambique, started to function in April 2002. It was set up by a private entrepreneur with a one-year low-interest (18 per cent) bank loan, which was guaranteed by the government cashew institute, INCAJU. The factory was designed with the help of TechnoServe, a USAID-financed NGO which aims to support entrepreneurial women and men in poor rural areas. Cashew is processed using the steaming method and semi-mechanical cutting machines. All the equipment, including ovens, has been manufactured locally, and the factory itself was reconstructed from a ruined building. It is intended that each year, the factory's output will increase towards its total capacity of 1,000 tons of raw cashew per year. In 2002, the factory began by processing 120 tons and employed 70 workers. The kernels produced are graded and vacuum-packed for export. The Dutch NGO, SNV, assisted the owner to contact a Dutch buyer who operates from Rotterdam and exports to various parts of the world.

Workers receive a free meal at work and, according to their contracts, have access to health assistance, paid annual holidays, and severance pay in case of professional illness or work accidents. A trade union has been set up and a crèche has been constructed in a clean, sheltered area where mothers can arrange for someone to look after their children (but with no provision of food or trained child-carers as in the old government-owned factories). The owner of the Namige factory has recently set up a second factory, and two more similar factories have been set up by other entrepreneurs in the province.

In India, women dominate the workforce in the cashew industry, operating cutting machines as well as peeling and grading the cashew. In this factory in Mozambique, only men are employed in the cutting section (43 men), while women predominate in the peeling section (32 women and 6 men), where the work is perceived as requiring dexterity and patience. Management explained this division in terms of women's own preferences, but the view was also expressed that women could not handle the cutting machine as well as men. There were mixed views from the women whom we interviewed: some did not want to burn their hands as it would affect their farming work, while others were willing to take any kind of work.

SNV, with support from TechnoServe, has further supported the Namige factory, by developing an initiative to set up small-scale processing units (so-called satellites) around the factory. One Mozambican NGO provides a training component for production and processing, and another provides a micro-finance component. The owner of the factory buys the produce from the small units. In the first year of the programme (2002–3), three units were set up, each with a capacity to process 24 tons of raw cashew. The units buy the raw cashews, steam, crack, dry, and peel them, and pack them for transport to the factory. In the factory, the nuts are sorted, graded, and packed for export. The owner of the factory is responsible for finding the buyers. The Dutch buyer can absorb high volumes of processed nuts for export to various parts of the world. The owner is building up the factory towards maximum capacity, while also out-sourcing the initial, labour-intensive stages of processing.

To minimise risks of management failure and test technical and economic viability, the first three units are run by individuals (two men and one woman) who have an entrepreneurial background and experience in marketing cashew. The idea is that if the units show viability, less experienced individuals, interest groups, associations, or family groups can be given the opportunity to run future units. A total of 21 units is foreseen for the first three years of the programme, with each unit employing about 12 people.

The satellites initiative has the potential to increase the quantity of the processed nuts, as well as generating employment for local people. In these cases, the chain becomes much shorter, minimising the number of intermediaries between producer and exporter, and adding value locally. This is a positive initiative, which should provide greater benefits to rural communities than the more typical chains, although small intermediary traders may lose out. However, it remains to be seen whether the satellite units are economically viable. At present, the Namige factory owner and TechnoServe have some reservations about the financial sustainability of the satellite units, because quality (the appearance of the nuts) and productivity (the proportion of 'whole' nuts produced) have been low, and costs are seen to be high, while prices of kernels on the international market have remained low.

The Namige initiative provides an interesting example of a 'partnership' approach between government, NGOs, communities, and the private sector. Better wages and working conditions are provided for workers than in other factories. Because of the involvement of SNV, and the positive relationships that have been built up, the owner of the factory made an effort to have at least one satellite run by a woman, and is in the process of importing castor oil to protect the workers' hands, because it is more effective than the local oil. Better protection may mean that more women want to work in the cutting section, although it remains to be seen if management will encourage them to do so.

Implications for the corporate responsibility agenda

In the current context, unions are weak or non-existent in the cashew-processing sectors in both India and Mozambique. Given the need for cash and employment opportunities, workers and unions find themselves in relatively weak positions. Action to promote workers' rights is complex and should not restrict the livelihood opportunities of poor workers, nor raise labour costs, so livelihood opportunities for people with few choices are further reduced. In the Namige case, the union had only just been set up when the research was carried out. The employer wanted the union to mediate between management and workers: to explain to workers the constraints that he faced as a result of international prices and to assure them that profits from increased productivity would be shared with them. Unions have often failed to represent the interests of women workers adequately, and the development of strong and representative workers' organisations is an important counterweight to more powerful interests. It is too early to say if the union in the Namige factory will develop in this way.

Governments have an essential role to play in protecting workers' rights and interests, particularly where unions and other civil society organisations are weak. Tri-partite discussions between employers, government, and workers' representatives at the national level should inform minimum-wage agreements and minimum working conditions. The researchers have suggested that the government should monitor compliance with minimum wages, or set up multi-stakeholder groups, including NGOs, to carry out this work.

In the 'better practice' that we have described in this paper, the Namige case illustrates the potentially important role of

86

support from NGOs working with government and business. However, this case is an exception, and gender inequalities persist in the benefits derived from employment within this initiative, since men are still in the higher-paid, more secure positions. Companies currently take advantage of gender inequalities, where women are assumed to be 'secondary earners', more willing to accept lower wages for their work, or perceived to be less skilled at some tasks than others.

Cashew nuts are considered a luxury food product, and a host of quality requirements is increasingly applied by the USA and Europe. There are indications that hygiene, safety, and improvements in working conditions will become more important elements to certification. However, the investment needed to upgrade conditions for certification is often costly, particularly for small businesses. It is usually the workers of larger companies, particularly those dealing with branded products, who benefit from higher labour standards associated with certification or codes of conduct.

Conclusion

Campaigners for greater corporate responsibility often focus on achieving 'win-wins', where improved social or environmental performance leads to business benefits. Such incentives for higher standards come through several points of leverage, including consumer demand, civil society pressure, public sector enforcement, and conditions imposed by investors or buyers. But the case of cashew illustrates the danger of a 'race to the bottom' when companies operating in liberalising sectors face few, if any, of these incentives.

While the Namige case is an exceptional example of better practice, women workers in this sector still face deteriorating wages, working conditions, and discrimination.

This case illustrates the potential for collaboration between government, NGOs, and employers for improvements in wages and working conditions in one location. It has even demonstrated some responses to issues raised by women workers, by setting up a crèche and providing better protection for workers' hands. However, these improvements are currently dependent on the awareness and goodwill of a particular employer/exporter and the work of a particular set of organisations working in that provincial location.

Cashew processors at the national level believe that greater profits are retained by salter-roaster companies and large retailers at the Northern end of the chain. The key challenge then, is to identify points of leverage along this end of the supply chain, where there is little pressure from consumers or buyers for higher labour standards. Until this happens, the costs of production will continue to be passed on to workers, and the Namige case may well remain an exceptional example of better practice.

Nazneen Kanji is Senior Research Associate in the Sustainable Agriculture and Rural Livelihoods Programme at IIED (International Institute for Environment and Development). She has been engaged in gender and development work for the past 20 years, and has lived and worked extensively in Africa. She has undertaken poverty and livelihood assessments in urban and rural contexts. nazneen.kanji@iied.org

References

Eapen, M., J. Jeyaranjan, K.N. Harilal, P. Swaminathan, and N. Kanji, N. (2004) 'Liberalisation, gender and livelihoods: the cashew nut case', IIED Working Paper 3: *India Phase 1: Revisiting the Cashew Industry*. Available on IIED website at www.iied.org/sarl/research/projects/t3proj01.html.

Kanji, N., C. Vijfhuizen, and S. Young (2002) 'Cashing in on Cashews. Policies, Production and Gender in Mozambique'. Paper presented at the 8th International Interdisciplinary Congress on Women, 21–26 July 2002, Kampala, Uganda.

Kanji, N., C. Vijfhuizen, C. Braga, and L. Artur (forthcoming) 'Cashing in on cashew nuts: women producers and factory workers in Mozambique', to be published in M. Carr (ed.) *Best Practices in Poverty Reduction: Linking informal economy women producers and workers to global markets*, London, UK: Commonwealth Secretariat.

Lindberg, A. (2001) *Experience and Identity: A historical account of class, caste and gender among cashew workers of Kerala*, Sweden: Lund University.

Vijfhuizen, C., C. Braga, L. Artur, and N. Kanji (2003a) 'Liberalisation, Gender and Livelihoods: the Cashew Nut Case', IIED Working Paper 1: *Mozambique Phase 1: the North* (English and Portuguese: available on IIED website at www.iied.org/sarl/research/projects/t3proj01.html)

Vijfhuizen, C., L. Artur, N. Kanji, and C. Braga (2003b) 'Liberalisation, Gender and Livelihoods: the Cashew Nut Case', IIED Working Paper 2: *Mozambique Phase 2: the South* (English and Portuguese: available on IIED website at www.iied.org/sarl/research/projects/t3proj01.html)

Resources

Compiled by Erin Leigh

Publications

Gender Mainstreaming in the Multilateral Trading System: a handbook for policy-makers and other stakeholders (2003) Mariama Williams, The Commonwealth Secretariat, Marlborough House, Pall Mall, London SW1Y 5HX.
http://publications.thecommonwealth.org/

This publication is an essential resource for understanding and integrating gender analysis into multilateral trade. Williams begins with a general description of the multilateral trade system and then considers it from a gender perspective. Various key aspects of the multilateral trading system are then addressed, including agriculture, services, investment, and intellectual property rights. The author presents strategies for integrating a gender perspective into the multilateral system, and an analysis of the content of the system itself.

'Global Trade Expansion and Liberalisation: Gender Issues and Impacts' (1998) Marzia Fontana, Susan Joekes, and Rachel Masika, BRIDGE, Institute of Development Studies University of Sussex, Brighton BN1 9RE, UK.
www.ids.ac.uk/bridge
Also available online at
www.ids.ac.uk/bridge/re42.pdf

The authors present a general analysis of trade expansion and liberalisation and show how these affect women's livelihoods. Usefully, the report provides a review of existing research, and its gaps. It also includes case studies from the Caribbean, South Asia, and Africa. The report then provides an overview of mechanisms that can be used to enforce labour standards and human rights alongside trade liberalisation. It concludes with a consideration of policy implications.

'Towards Monitoring Mutual Trade – Gender Links' (2002) Irene van Staveren, Institute of Social Studies, PO Box 29776, 2502 LT The Hague, The Netherlands.
www.iss.nl/
Also available online at
http://adlib.iss.nl/adlib/uploads/wp/wp358.pdf

This paper provides a worthwhile contribution to the gender and trade literature. First, it includes a literature review on gender and trade. This review is split into three themes: macro-economic effects, labour-market effects, and socio-economic effects. Van Staveren then proposes a set of 14 indicators to measure the impact of trade internationally, or to monitor bilateral trade agreements. The paper finishes with a case study of a bilateral agreement between Europe and some South American countries (Mercosur countries).

Gender Focus on the WTO (1999) Eva Haxton and Claes Olsson (eds.), Global Publications Foundation, Stiftelsen Global Kunskap, Box 1221, S-751 42, Uppsala, Sweden.
www.globalpublications.org/eng/indexeng.html

This collection of articles addresses the need to incorporate gender equality into the WTO, and presents case studies and strategies to do this. Articles cover a range of issues, including textiles, the environment, and human rights.

'Transformation, Participation, Gender Justice: Feminist Challenges in a Globalised Economy' (2003) Mandy Macdonald, Women in Development Europe (WIDE), rue de la Science 10, 1000 Brussels, Belgium.
www.eurosur.org/wide/

This report from WIDE's Annual Conference 2003, hosted by the WIDE Austria in Vienna, 23–24 May 2003, offers new insights into the present complex political, economic, and social dynamics of world trade by analysing the negative consequences of these trends for women worldwide. It suggests feminist strategies and alternatives to meet the numerous challenges posed by the neo-liberal system.

'Gender Issues in Agricultural Market Liberalisation' (1996) Sally Baden, BRIDGE, Institute of Development Studies, University of Sussex, Brighton BN1 9RF, United Kingdom.
www.ids.ac.uk/bridge
Also available online at
www.ids.ac.uk/bridge/Reports/re42c.pdf

Baden presents an analysis of gender in agricultural market liberalisation. While this paper is relatively technical, it offers useful suggestions on areas where further research is needed, and ways of considering various processes related to agricultural market liberalisation from a gender perspective.

'At Work and at Home: A Comparative Perspective', TMD Discussion Paper No. 110 (2003) Marzia Fontana, Trade and Macroeconomics Division, International Food Policy Research Institute (IFPRI), 2033 K St. NW, Washington, DC 20006, USA.
www.ifpri.org
Note: One hard copy is available free of charge by emailing IFPRI-TM@cgiar.org

This is a technical document which uses a gendered social-accounting matrix and computable general equilibrium model (CGE) to analyse the varying effects that trade has on women, depending on their particular context and circumstances. It compares conditions in Bangladesh and Zambia to examine the impact of trade on gender inequality, depending on context-specific culture and labour-market characteristics. It explores other economic models, the strengths of the CGE model, and suggests further research.

'Gender Mainstreaming in Trade and Industry: A Reference Manual for Governments and other Stakeholders' (2000) Louise O'Regan, The Commonwealth Secretariat, Marlborough House, Pall Mall, London SW1Y 5HX.
http://publications.thecommonwealth.org/

This main focus of this manual is on gender mainstreaming within Ministries of Trade and related government agencies, but the text would be useful in other contexts. It promotes women's advancement through strategies to incorporate their concerns on a regularly monitored cycle. It also includes suggestions on advancing gender equality in the private sector.

Rigged Rules and Double Standards: Trade, Globalisation, and the Fight Against Poverty (2002) Oxfam GB, 274 Banbury Road, Oxford, OX2 7DZ.
www.oxfam.org.uk/publications/
Also available online at
www.maketradefair.com/assets/english/report_english.pdf

This comprehensive report analyses the nature of international trade, and the way in which the current regulations favour the needs and economies of rich countries and discriminate against poor countries. It is a call to action to challenge the current system that results in the rich getting richer, and the poor getting poorer.

Global Woman: Nannies, Maids, and Sex Workers in the New Economy (2003) Barbara Ehrenreich and Arlie Russell Hochschild (eds.) Metropolitan Books, Henry Holt and Company, Inc., 115 West 18th Street, New York, NY 10011, USA.
www.henryholt.com/metropolitanbooks.htm

Global Woman is a collection of articles relating to the experiences of women migrant workers. It analyses trends that rely on migrant women workers to support rich country care economies, to the detriment of their own families. Topics covered include the situation of Mexican nannies in Los Angeles, and Thai girls in Japanese brothels.

Doing the Dirty Work: The Global Politics of Domestic Labour (2000) Bridget Anderson
Zed Books, 7 Cynthia Street, London N1 9JF / Room 400, 175 Fifth Avenue, New York, NY 100010, USA.
www.zedbooks.co.uk

This study examines migrant domestic work in the North. In doing so, issues of gender, race, and class are raised. It challenges the image of a homogeneous woman with a single set of needs. Instead it identifies differences in women's interests, and describes the way in which migrant women are exploited to advance other women's status. The book, based on original research, is a useful introduction to the issues.

Gender, Trafficking, and Slavery (2002) Rachel Masika (ed.) Oxfam GB, 274 Banbury Road, Oxford, OX2 7DZ.
www.oxfam.org.uk/publications/

This collection of articles addresses the illegal 'trade' of people across borders. While no contribution explicitly considers economic trade and trafficking, there is an analysis of the impact of economic globalisation, including the agenda of trade liberalisation, on the lives of women, men, and children.

Partners in Change: Stories of Women's Collectives (2002) Global Alliance Against Traffic in Women (GAATW), PO Box 36, Bangkok Noi Post Office, Bangkok 10700, Thailand
www.gaatw.org

Partners in Change presents a series of interviews conducted by local activists or GAATW staff with women's groups in India, Bangladesh, Cambodia, Vietnam, Thailand, and Indonesia. It highlights women's capacity to organise, and improve their own and others' lives. Also available is 'Partners in Change: A Report of the Conference', 2002, a three-day conference organised by GAATW.

Promoting Gender Equality. A Resource Kit for Trade Unions (2002) International Labour Organization (ILO), ILO Publications, 4 route des Morillons, CH-1211 Geneva 22, Switzerland. pubvente@ilo.org
www.ilo.org
Available online at
www.ilo.org/public/english/employment/gems/eeo/tu/tu_toc.htm

The ILO has produced a collection of eight booklets as tools to help trade unions to promote gender equality, both within unions and through their work. The booklets cover topics such as working with diversity, promoting women workers' rights, and promoting gender equality through collective bargaining.

Women Workers: Reaching for the Sky. Trade Unions and the Beijing Platform for Action (2000) Kate Holman, International Confederation of Free Trade Unions (ICFTU). Available online at
www.icftu.org/www/pdf/womensky.pdf

Holman's publication traces the progress made in promoting gender equality within and through trade unions, especially as recommended by the Beijing Platform for Action. A large number of CFTU country assessments are included in the document. This is followed by a broader analysis of governments' commitments and progress on the platform, and the issues that are most pertinent to trade unions, including migrant women workers, the informal sector, prostitution, and more. Underscoring all of this are emerging and increasing barriers to gender equality, including violence against women, the gap between the rich and poor, and exploitation in the workplace.

Journals

World Development 28/7 (2000) Caren Grown, Diane Elson and Nilufer Cagatay (eds.), Elsevier, Customer Service Department, PO Box 211, 1000 AE Amsterdam, The Netherlands.
www.elsevier.com

This special issue of World Development is about growth, trade, finance, and gender inequalities. It is edited by members of the International Working Group on Gender, Macroeconomics and International Economics, as part of a larger initiative to explore ways to apply gender analysis to macro-economics, both theoretically and practically. The issue is divided into three sections: (1) gender, inequality, growth, and trade liberalisation; (2) gender inequality and financial liberalisation; and (3) gender relations and production in agricultural economies. The contents are challenging to those unfamiliar with economics, but make an important contribution to the field of gender and economics in development.

IDS Bulletin 32/3 (July 2001) Institute of Development Studies, Publications Office, IDS, University of Sussex, Brighton BN1 9RE.
www.ids.ac.uk/ids/bookshop/index.html

This issue of the IDS Bulletin is entitled 'The Value of Value Chains: Spreading the Gains of Globalisation'. It addresses value chains from numerous perspectives in 11 articles. Among these is an article by Stephanie Barrientos on 'Gender, flexibility, and global value chains' which considers (from a gender perspective) value chains in horticulture that link South Africa, Chile, and Europe.

Electronic resources

'Trade, Gender and Poverty' (2001) Nilufer Çagatay, United Nations Development Program (UNDP).
www.undp.org/mainundp/propoor/docs/pov_tradegenderpoverty_doc.pdf

Çagatay analyses the relationships between trade, poverty, and gender, considering their impact on gender inequalities, especially via employment, wages, and the care economy. It also looks at the impact of gender inequalities on trade itself. A valuable text for understanding the issues in an explicitly development-focused framework.

'Engendering International Trade: Concepts, Policy and Action' (1995) Lourdes Benería and Amy Lind, Gender, Science and Development Programme and the United Nations Development Fund for Women.
www.ifias.ca/gsd/beneria.contents.html

This paper presents the gender dimensions of trade, underpinned by a more general background on regional and global trade liberalisation. The gendered effects of trade on employment, price, and income are considered, demonstrating the need for context-specific analysis to understand the positive and negative effects on women. The paper then addresses particular sectors, industries, and regions from a gender perspective, and highlights emerging issues and areas for further research.

'Globalization and the Informal Economy: How Global Trade and Investment Impact on the Working Poor' (2001) Marilyn Carr and Martha Chen, International Labour Organization (ILO).
www.wiego.org/papers/ilo_chen.pdf

Carr and Chen analyse the growing informal economy under global trade liberalisation.

They explore the opportunities and barriers that this growing sector presents to women, both self-employed and wage workers. Working areas covered include fashion, non-traditional agricultural exports, and shea butter, while regions covered are Asia, Africa, and Latin America and the Caribbean.

'Trade, Sustainable Development and Gender' (1999) United Nations Conference on Trade and Development.
www.unctad.org/en/docs/poedm_m78.en.pdf

A collection of more than 40 papers prepared in support of the themes discussed at the Pre-UNCTAD Expert Workshop. Written predominantly by experts from developing countries, and countries in transition, they present research and analysis on the connections between trade, sustainable development and gender, recommending ways in which UNCTAD could work on all three in conjunction. Both conceptual and country case studies are presented from Africa, South Asia, Eastern Europe, South America, and North America. A useful and comprehensive resource.

'Gender, International Trade and the Trade Policy Review Mechanism: Conceptual Reference Points for UNCTAD' (2002) Barbara Evers, Gapresearch.org, IDS.
www.gapresearch.org/governance/BE%20evers%20unctad%20paper1.pdf

This document considers particular issues of importance to UNCTAD with respect to gender and trade. The author begins by examining the connections between economic policy and gender, before considering trade liberalisation more deeply. Examples of specific issues include gender inequality and agriculture, the need for trade mechanisms and policies to understand women's work burdens, and the weakened ability of the state to support commitments made to gender equality in a liberalised context.

'Analysis of the Free Trade Area of the Americas Text from a Gender Perspective' (2003) Marceline White and Alexandra Spieldoch, Hemispheric Social Alliance.
www.stitchonline.org/archives/WEAnalysisperspective.pdf

White and Spieldoch have undertaken a gender analysis of the second draft of the Free Trade of the Americas (FTAA) text. In this brief paper, key concerns are raised about the potential for the agreement to further marginalise women in particular and poor people more generally. Concerns raised by the authors include the liberalisation of agriculture at the expense of subsistence agriculture, and the privatisation of services, which makes them increasingly expensive and inaccessible. They conclude with recommendations to show how policy and practice in each area of concern could be made more gender-sensitive and pro-poor.

'The NEPAD, Gender and the Poverty Trap' (2002) Zo Randriamaro, Gender and Economic Reforms in Africa Programme (GERA).
www.twnafrica.org/gera.asp

Randriamaro analyses the New Partnership for Africa's Development (NEPAD) from a gender perspective. She questions its ability to reduce poverty in the region while it maintains a predominantly neo-liberal framework (which includes trade liberalisation). She argues that the NEPAD, with its dominant economic focus on neo-liberalisation, is blind to gender and other social concerns, and will have a detrimental impact on both women and men.

'Women in Economic Decision Making: A Study on the Barriers to Career Progression' (2003) Jenny Kimmis, Institute of Development Studies (IDS).
www.ids.ac.uk/ids/global/finance/pdfs/WEcoStudyFinal.pdf

This study presents a review of the literature on women in economics, and on women in management. It is supported by 12 interviews with women in different levels of decision-making in the field of economics. This is a valuable contribution to understanding how women are restricted from advancing in economics, and what women and organisations are doing to address these restrictions.

'Engendering International Trade: Gender Equality in a Global World' (no date) European Women's Lobby.
www.womenlobby.org/Document.asp?DocID=220&tod=4141
This brief primer from the European Women's Lobby outlines in a clear and accessible manner the particular impacts of trade on women, both positive and negative. It covers various pertinent topics and provides recommendations targeted at the EU and beyond. Topics covered include poverty, labour, trafficking, migration, and women's family life.

'The TRIPS and Public Health Debate: An Overview' (2001) Mariama Williams, International Gender and Trade Network (IGTN).
www.coc.org/pdfs/coc/TRIPSandHealth.pdf
This accessible article, with technical terms defined in the footnotes and text, provides an understanding of the key issues relating the World Trade Organisation's (WTO) agreement on the Trade-Related Aspects of Intellectual Property Rights (TRIPS). The core issue are the obstacles posed to Southern nations which need to acquire cheap drugs for illnesses, especially HIV/AIDS.

Tools and websites

'Gender and Trade Indicators' (2002) Irene van Staveren, Women in Development Europe (WIDE).
www.genderandtrade.net/Europe/InformationSH.pdf

This brief WIDE information sheet suggests how indicators can be used to analyse the relationships between gender and trade, both on a country-to-country level and on a trading-bloc level. Three sets of indicators are presented: situational, political will, and dynamic indicators. The use of these indicators is then demonstrated in various capacities, from identifying the consistency between gender and trade policy, to identifying the need to incorporate gender concerns into policy.

'Gender and International Trade: an Annotated Bibliography' (2002) Chantal Blouin, Status of Women Canada.
http://collection.nlc-bnc.ca/100/200/301/swc-cfc/gender_intl_trade-e/html/index_e.html
This annotated bibliography identifies literature that is both Canada-specific and international. It covers a range of related topics including gender and trade generally; trade and labour standards; trade and migration; intellectual property and aboriginal women in Canada; trade and health care; trade and human rights; and trade and women entrepreneurs.

UNIFEM Gender and Trade Website
www.unifem.org/trade
UNIFEM's website provides accessible resources for understanding the relationship between gender and trade. It includes a 'situational analysis' of a range of issues related to gender and trade, such as intellectual property rights, trade in services, and women's employment.

Make Trade Fair
www.maketradefair.com
This is Oxfam's trade campaign website. It contains a report entitled 'Trading Away Our Rights: Women working in global supply chains' report (see the article by Kidder and Raworth in this collection). In addition, it provides opportunities to learn more about fair trade and to take action in support of the campaign.

Focus on Trade – Can Trade Generate Development for Women? KULU Women and Development. www.kulu.dk/Financing/Seminar/introduction .htm

The Focus on Trade website is the result of a seminar on the importance of gender and trade in relation to the UN Conference Financing for Development (FfD) (2002). It includes workshop reports and present-ations from a variety of regional perspec-tives including Africa, Asia, the Caribbean, Central and Eastern Europe, and the Newly Independent States (CEE/NIS).

The International Confederation of Free Trade Unions (ICFTU)
www.icftu.org
ICFTU, established in 1949, has 233 affiliated organisations in 152 countries and territories on all five continents, with a membership of 150 million. One of its concerns is gender equality, and you can find gender and trade union publications and resources on this website, including the 'Organising Campaign Kit: Women for Unions: Unions for Women' and 'Positive Action Programme for Women and Development'.

Organisations

International Gender and Trade Network, IGTN Secretariat, 1225 Otis Street, NE, Washington, DC 20017, USA. Tel: 202 635 2757 ext. 128; Fax: 202 832 9494
secretariat@coc.org
www.genderandtrade.net

This network consists of seven regional networks (Africa, Asia, Caribbean, Europe, Latin America, North America, and Pacific) of women involved in research, advocacy, and economic literacy on issues of trade and development.

Caribbean Association for Feminist Research and Action (CAFRA), PO Bag 442, Tunapuna Post Office, Tunapuna, Trinidad and Tobago. Tel: (868) 663 8670; (868) 662 1231; (868) 662 6472; Fax: 868 663 6482
cafrainfo@wow.net

CAFRA is a regional network of feminists, individual researchers, activists, and women's organisations which defines feminist politics as a matter of both consciousness and action. CAFRA, committed to understanding the relationship between the oppression of women and other forms of oppression in the society, is working actively for change.

The Gender and Economic Reforms in Africa Programme (GERA), PO Box AN 19452 , Accra, North Ghana. Tel: (233) 21 511189/503669; Fax: (233) 21 511188
gera@twnafrica.org
www.twnafrica.org/gera.asp

The Gender and Economic Reforms in Africa (GERA) programme is a pan-African research and advocacy programme, established in 1996 by women from across Africa in order to influence economic policies and decision-making processes in Africa from a gender perspective. Committed to gender equality and economic justice, the programme supports African women to undertake a variety of African-designed policy research and advocacy projects that meet country- and region-specific needs. Since 1996, GERA has supported 16 action-research projects in 11 sub-Saharan African countries.

Development Alternatives with Women for a New Era (DAWN), PO Box 13124, Suva, Fiji. Tel/Fax: (679) 314 770
admin@dawn.org.fj
www.dawn.org.fj

DAWN began in 1984, on the eve of the international conferences marking the end of the UN Decade for Women, when a group of feminists from the South with similar visions prepared a platform document for that event and held a number of workshops at the NGO Forum in Nairobi. DAWN's platform document, *Development, Crises and Alternative Visions: Third World Women's Perspectives* (Monthly Review Press 1987), written by Gita Sen and Caren Grown, was a Southern feminist critique of three decades of development. One of DAWN's programme themes is the 'Political Economy of Globalisation'.

Women's International Coalition for Economic Justice (WICEJ), New York, NY 10040, USA.
info@wicej.org;
www.wicej.org

WICEJ is an international coalition, representing organisations in all regions of the globe. It works to link gender with macro-economic policy in international inter-government policy-making arenas, from a human rights perspective. It utilises an integrated feminist analysis which links the multiplicity of systems that oppress women, and it recognises the diversity of women's experience, determined by race, ethnicity, class, national origin, citizenship status, and other factors.

Women Working Worldwide, MMU Manton Building, Rosamond Street West, Manchester M15 6LL, UK.
info@women-ww.org
www.poptel.org.uk/women-ww/

Women Working Worldwide is a small UK voluntary organisation working with a global network of women-worker organisations. It began in 1983, when a group of researchers and activists came together to organise a conference on women and the international division of labour. Its aim is to support the rights of women workers in an increasingly globalised economy in which women are used as a source of cheap and flexible labour. The focus has been on industries which have relocated to the developing world, particularly the textile and garment industry. Work is also now taking place on fresh produce supply chains.

Women's Edge, 1825 Connecticut Avenue NW, Suite 800, Washington, DC 20009, USA.
Tel: (202) 884 8396
edge@womensedge.org
www.womensedge.org

Women's lack of participation in economic and trade policies stunts economies, holds back countries, and makes the goal of ending poverty nearly impossible. To address this, the Women's Edge Coalition, a non-partisan organisation, was created in 1998 to advocate for the needs of millions of women and poor people around the world left destitute and desperate by unfair trade policies. The Coalition offers positive alternatives to current policies and pushes for innovative aid programmes to ensure that women around the world are not forgotten, but given access to the trade negotiation process. By revising the process of economic and trade negotiations, both trade promoters and the world's poorest women benefit.

Maquila Solidarity Network (MSN), 606 Shaw Street, Toronto, Ontario, Canada M6G 3L6.
Tel: (416) 532 8584; Fax: (416) 532 7688
info@maquilasolidarity.org
www.maquilasolidarity.org

The Maquila Solidarity Network is a Canadian network which promotes solidarity with groups in Mexico, Central America, and Asia that are organising in *maquiladora* factories and export-processing zones to improve conditions and win a living wage. In a global economy it is essential that groups in the North and South work together for employment with dignity, fair wages and working conditions, and healthy workplaces and communities.

Printed in the United Kingdom
by Lightning Source UK Ltd.
115133UKS00001B/3-104

9 780855 985325